THINK LIKE A WALL STREET ANALYST

Murphy's Law - Lessons from Covering Airline Stocks

Table of Contents

Forward	1
Industry Structure Defines the Game	5
Finding a Business with a Sustainable Edge	17
Cycles Come in Many Forms	29
Big Data	45
Valuation – Good Companies are not Always Good Stocks	61
Avoiding Psychological Mistakes	77
Elements of a Good Stock Pitch	87
Thematic Research – Stories Drive Stocks	95
Roles of an Analyst	113

Forward

Have you ever been on a group tour and become annoyed at a person who kept asking the guide questions? I confess that jerk is sometimes me, though in my defense I always wait until others have run out of their questions. I also make sure my questions are shorter than the answers, and I rationalize to myself that the guide prefers a give-and-take more than a one-way dialogue. If you are also the type of person who asks a lot of questions, consider becoming a security analyst. [Curiosity is probably a defining characteristic of a Wall Street analyst.]

With that introduction, you should not be surprised that this is a book of questions rather than answers. The purpose of the book is to give the investor a framework for analyzing companies. Capital markets are critical for corporations as well, and I also hope this book gives corporate managers and employees perspective on how Wall Street views their businesses.

I have divided the book up into a series of questions to identify factors that make good or bad investments. In my experience, I find that I learn much more about a company or industry when a stock pick goes wrong than when it goes right. One of the advantages of covering airline stocks for 25 years at Goldman Sachs and Bank of America is that the airline sector provides so many examples of what can go wrong. I was also fortunate to have 45 smart and engaging analysts teach me about their sectors during my years helping manage BofA Global Research.

> Warren Buffett once said, "Buy stock in businesses that are so wonderful that an idiot can run them; because sooner or later one will."

The first section of the book discusses industry structure and aims to help investors identify the characteristics that make good or bad businesses. Timing matters, and the next section deals with cycles, including economic, commodity, credit, housing, inventory, product cycles, and even the life cycle of a stock. The section seeks to help investors anticipate cycles and highlights some leading indicators of industry demand, pricing, and profits.

Because the world is now flooded with data, I have devoted a section to the variety of data sources that can provide investors with market insights - both conventional and unconventional. This section also includes views regarding the strengths and weaknesses of quantitative analysis, and the following chapter reviews the pros and cons of various valuation methodologies.

> "Know thy enemy and know yourself; in a hundred battles you will never be defeated."

Sun Tzu's quote demonstrates the importance of psychology in the market. In this chapter, we'll discuss investor biases and ways to recognize and/or avoid one's own biases and risk parameters.

Successful Wall Street analysts not only have to be right, but they have to convince others as well. Often that requires a good story teller. The final section deals with the dos and don'ts of a good research report, tips on modeling, and key themes to currently consider when investing.

I will end this introduction with a rhetorical question.

What do capitalism, democracy, and nature have in common and how can that make one a better stock picker?

The characteristic that most commonly comes to mind is self-interest. Darwin's theories of natural selection are based on the premise that organisms want to survive and multiply. When pundits say "It's the economy, stupid", they are assuming people vote for the candidate that will make them better off, and capitalism is based on the view that people will make goods that will generate wealth and buy goods that bring them satisfaction. I'm an optimist and I believe people are not quite that selfish, but those assumptions are certainly a good starting point.

However, the real strength of these systems is not based on their appeal to self-interest, but their built-in learning mechanisms. In nature, organisms that adapt to changes in the environment (including competition from other organisms) thrive and multiply while those organisms that do not evolve die out. In a healthy democracy, politicians who deliver their promises get reelected and those who are ineffective get voted out. Winston Churchill said that you can always count on the Americans to do the right thing after they have tried everything else. This backhanded compliment has some hidden, unintended wisdom. Americans do keep trying until they get it right although as evident in racial and gender rights, progress can be agonizingly slow and require persistence from those seeking justice.

Capitalism has many pitfalls, but capitalism's strength is that the markets provide a continual, relatively unbiased learning mechanism. Companies that provide services and products desired by consumers thrive, but success draws competition to keep the initial winners on their toes. The stock market awards good businesses inexpensive capital for them to expand and starves bad businesses of capital. Yes, as in nature, companies go out of business and people suffer, but in America new businesses are always starting up to take their place. Command economies fail, not because their leaders aren't smart, but because no one is smart enough to navigate all the possible outcomes, and socialist economies lack the feedback loop to quickly learn from mistakes.

What is the lesson for investors? Just as the stock market is continually reassessing equity values, investors must constantly question their own assumptions. A good analyst is not afraid of being wrong, but is afraid of staying wrong. An analyst must always question his thesis every day and know how to adapt when a strategy is no longer working. The chapter on market psychology offers some tips to counter our natural stubbornness.

.

Industry Structure Defines the Game

> "The worst sort of business is one that grows rapidly, requires significant capital to engender the growth, and then earns little or no money. Think airlines. Here a durable competitive advantage has proven elusive ever since the days of the Wright Brothers. Indeed, if a farsighted capitalist had been present at Kitty Hawk, he would have done his successors a huge favor by shooting Orville down."
>
> -- Warren Buffett, in the 2007 Berkshire Hathaway shareholder letter

The airline business over time has lost more money than it has made. What has made the airline business such a bad business for shareholders (consumers certainly have benefited, labor has benefited with compensation well above the national average, and airlines have created jobs for travel-related business) and what lesson does that provide for other industries? Throughout my career following airlines, I was always struck by the fact that the executives themselves complained about irrational behavior by their competitors, yet it would be hard for many CEOs to match the sheer intelligence of Southwest Airlines' Herb Kelleher, the creativity of American's Bob Crandall, or the common sense of Continental's Gordon Bethune. So how can an industry of intelligent executives result in a collection of seemingly irrational players? An analysis of a business from a game theory provides an answer. A good way to start is to play the game, Prisoners' dilemma.

		Prisoner 2	
		Keep Mum	Rat
Prisoner 1	Mum	3 years for both	15 years Prisoner 1 1 year Prisoner 2
	Rat	1 year Prisoner 1 15 years Prisoner 2	10 years for both

Imagine two gang members are in separate cells and cannot communicate with each other. The police give each prisoner the following choice - confess while betraying your partner or maintain both of your innocence. If both prisoners remain mum, the prosecutor has enough evidence to convict both of them of a lesser crime with a punishment of 3 years in jail. If only one prisoner betrays the other, the stool pigeon's plea bargain will reduce his sentence to 1 year while the other prisoner gets a 15-year sentence. However, if both prisoners rat on each other, then the value of the plea bargain is diminished and both prisoners receive a 10-year sentence.

The outsider can see that the best possible combined outcome for both prisoners is to stand by their confederate, remain mum, and accept punishment for the lesser crime. Together they will receive 6 years of prison—3 years apiece. The worst collective outcome is for both to be disloyal and receive a combined 20 years of prison. If only one prisoner betrays the other, the total of the two prison terms is 16 years—1 for the betrayer and 15 for the betrayed.

So, cooperation appears to be the most logical outcome on a combined basis. But sitting in their separate cells, the prisoners have a different perspective. If one fears the other will confess, then betraying one's partner as well will result in 5 fewer years of prison (10 years instead of 15). But even if one thinks their partner will remain true, betraying the other partner will create a better outcome (1 year instead of 3) So no matter what one thinks their partner will decide, the prisoner determines that betrayal creates a better outcome than loyalty. An individually rational decision has created a collectively irrational outcome.

"C'mon, c'mon — it's either one or the other."

In the 1980s, the airlines provided many examples of losing due to prisoners' dilemma. How can it make sense for an airline that doesn't earn its capital to purchase aircraft for growth? For one, adding another plane lowers an airline's average unit costs given that existing infrastructure costs are now spread over more flights. Second, bringing in newer planes lowers the average age of the fleet and improves its efficiency. Lastly, newly hired employees lower the average wage level of an airline because airline wages rise with seniority, and in the 1980s, airline managements negotiated lower pay scales for new hires. In addition, a larger airline is more attractive to its customers by providing more direct and connecting opportunities, a loyalty program that can accumulate miles faster as well as offer more opportunities to use miles, and a more attractive corporate discount program. Consequently, by improving both their relative cost and revenue position, an airline comes to the conclusion that growth will improve its competitive position even as they decry other airlines' expansion plans. When Carl Icahn acquired TWA, he refused to play the irrational expansion game, but still ended up suffering from industry overcapacity while becoming a less relevant industry participant.

Other examples of airlines falling into the prisoners' dilemma trap involve amenities, pricing, and distribution. Prior to deregulation and even during the early days of deregulation, airlines competed on service, but even in more recent times, there have been competition for business travelers regarding amenities, particularly on international flights. Airlines in the 1990s began offering fully reclining seats to their international customers to win share. However, lie-flat seats take up valuable real estate on planes. The first airlines that shifted to the larger seats captured a higher share of the premium traveler, but with all airlines eventually matching, the airlines premium cabins now have higher cost per seat than before, and, therefore, lower margins.

In the 1980s, the airlines also competed to win travel agency businesses by offering higher commissions to agencies that shifted share. However, commission hikes can easily be matched and the end result was little change in share, but commission rates doubled to 8% of revenues. I remember Texas Air cutting fares in Dallas because the impact would be greater on American than Continental, only to result in American retaliating by cutting fares in Continental's Houston hub. I also remember American airlines advocating for stricter maintenance rules because the cost increase would be incrementally greater on competitors. Both are examples of an industry losing at prisoners' dilemma.

Factors Contributing to Prisoners' Dilemma

Airlines are not the only industry with unfavorable competitive dynamics. OPEC has been a notoriously poorly functioning cartel. Despite industry consolidation, rental companies still earn subpar returns as do wireless service providers and cruise lines. Even the duopoly of Boeing and Airbus deliver unattractive returns on assets. Insurance, and particularly reinsurance, has historically suffered big ups and downs as capital flowed in and out of the market. In metals, steel and aluminum margins are highly cyclical and typically low. In real estate, senior housing has underperformed, and within tech, storage margins are generally low. Within ground transportation, rail profits have proven to be stronger and less cyclical than trucks.

So, what are the factors that contribute to creating an industry with unfavorable competitive dynamics and can these factors be changed? In order of importance, I would cite the following:

1) Marginal economics.
2) Number of industry participants.
3) Substitutability.
4) Barriers to entry.
5) Asset life.
6) Ability to monitor cheating.
7) Speed of feedback loop.

Marginal Economics

As touched on earlier, the marginal cost of an airline adding a flight is lower than the average cost. With infrastructure (airport, distribution, headquarters) in place, flying a plane an extra hour or two a day creates relatively low incremental costs (added fuel, labor, wear) so increasing capacity tends to lower an airline's average cost, thus, improving their competitive position. Industries that are overly incentivized to add capacity have trouble raising prices and boosting returns.

In general, industries with high levels of fixed costs have less favorable competitive dynamics. With wells and pipelines already in place, oil companies' marginal cost of output is much lower than their average cost per barrel. The incremental cost of adding a new rental car driver, cruise passenger, or wireless customer are low so the service provider can apparently justify a lower price to capture the incremental demand. The marginal cost for traditional steel mills (as opposed to mini-mills which use scrap steel instead of iron) and aluminum smelters are also low, leading to higher volatility of prices when utilizations fall. Furthermore, the chunkiness of costs can understate the marginal costs of output. For example, an incremental flight may have low costs, but eventually you need more planes, more gates, more maintenance hangars, more training facilities, and the greater complexity requires more systems as well. Despite seemingly greater economies of scale, large airlines typically have higher rather than lower unit costs compared to small airlines.

Marginal economics can involve revenues as well as costs. For airlines, adding a flight to a hub (i.e., Greensboro to Atlanta) not only brings incremental revenue to the Greensboro-Atlanta leg, but also adds revenue to the more than 200 other destinations that Delta offers passengers out of Atlanta. Cruise lines often find that newly built ships with added amenities generate more revenues than the existing fleet. Networks create value in other industries as well. A hospitality chain with hotels across the world provides more opportunities for customers to benefit from loyalty programs and corporates to capitalize on discounts than chains with a narrower geography. By offering resorts in the Rockies, Canada and Northeast, Vail's ski season pass has become more attractive relative to single mountain resorts. Time-shares that can market a variety of locations also increase their appeal to vacationers. As with revenues, the marginal economics of revenue can be misleading. Despite their computerized revenue management systems, airlines that try to cut prices to stimulate demand in order to fill incremental supply, end up having to put existing seats on sale as well. A new cruise ship may end up cannibalizing demand from the legacy ships or at least make them look relatively less appealing.

More Players, Less Cooperation

If you played prisoner's dilemma just once, you'd be likely to rat on your opponent, but if you and the opponent were forced to play the game many times in succession, you both would quickly realize that cooperation would provide a better outcome than cheating. However, the more people that are playing, the tougher it is to reach a cooperative outcome.

OPEC was formed in recognition that oil nations needed to cooperate to curtail production, but OPEC has proven to be an ineffective oligopoly and largely relies on Saudi Arabia alone to manage supply. With so many players, each individual country feels that if its nation alone cheats, the overall member cooperation can hold. In the same vein, truckers have more difficulty than railroads in maintaining prices during periods of weak demand. There are thousands of truckers, but only a handful of railroads, and pricing becomes much more cutthroat with a greater number of participants. Industries have consolidated in nearly all parts of the US economy, which I believe has contributed to higher prices and corporate profit margins doubling over the past few decades.

As previously mentioned, a fragmented airline industry competed vigorously for travel agency share. Even though the number of airlines remained high in the 1990s, a series of mergers enabled airlines to dominate their hubs. With more than of 75% of the flights in a region being offered by one airline, travel agencies could no longer easily shift share. With less need to woo agents, airlines felt free to reduce agency incentives, and commission rates have plummeted to less than 1% as compared to more than 12% thirty years ago.

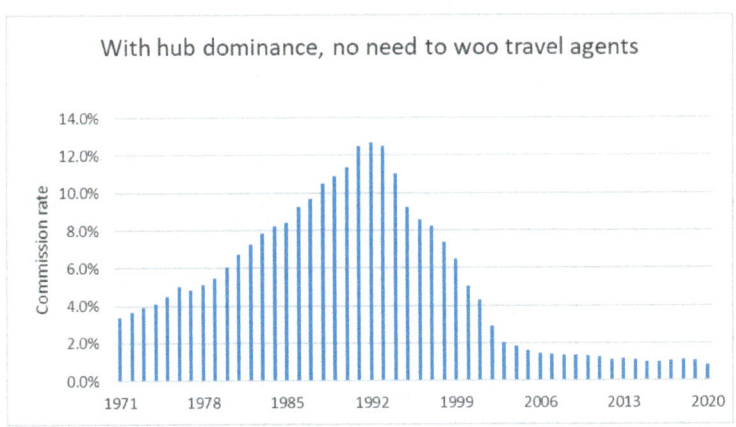

Similarly, with travelers having fewer options, airlines had less pressure to offer passenger amenities. Airlines began to put more rows on their planes, which lowered their unit costs at the expense of shrinking passenger legroom. Airlines also began to cut back on food costs, eliminating meals on many shorter flights. As a result, food costs per passenger are currently half of what they were thirty years ago, even before adjusting for inflation.

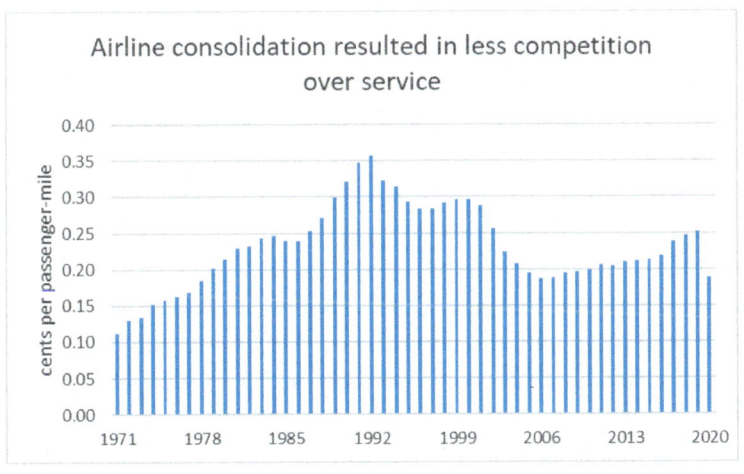

For an industry to behave cooperatively, there needs to be a way to monitor cheating. Transparency of pricing may be good for consumers, but transparency of supply is good for producers. OPEC has had difficulty enforcing member compliance because country production can be hard to monitor on a timely basis, particularly in less open economies. On the other hand, airlines have to post their schedules months in advance so industry discipline is easier to enforce.

New players, Less Cooperation

Just as more participants make cooperation more difficult to achieve, the introduction of new players resets the learning curve in prisoner's dilemma. A series of airline mergers created an industry oligopoly in the late 1980s and early 1990s. As the industry structure changed and regional concentration increased, territorial battles abated. When American, Delta, and United held 50% share of the Atlanta, Dallas, and Denver markets, the desire for hub dominance caused them to boost supply. As passenger share at these hubs approached 80%, the incentive to add supply to gain share diminished, and as airline capacity additions decelerated from high single-digit growth in the 1980s to low double-digit growth in the 1990s, industry pricing/returns began to improve.

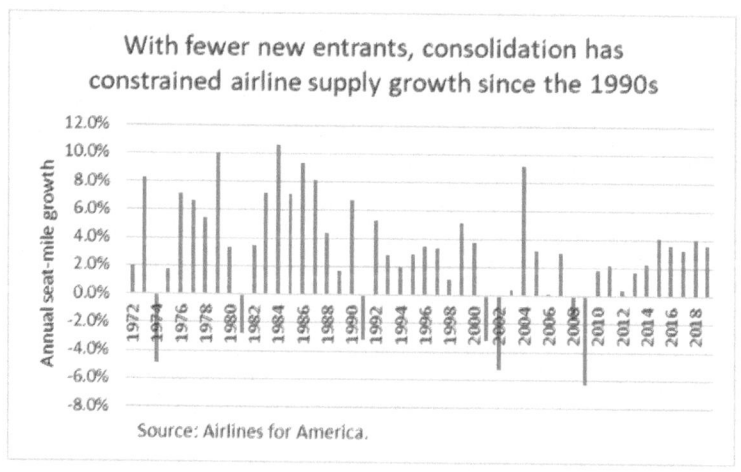

However, supply discipline proved ephemeral as the new entrants took advantage of the capacity restraint of their larger competitors. Initially, the aggressive expansion of low fare carriers had a modest effect on pricing dynamics, but as their share of the market expanded from 5% in 1990 to 15% in 2000, their impact on pricing intensified, and the airlines were once again plagued with excess supply. However, bankruptcies have helped narrow the legacy carriers' cost disadvantage and limitations on gates/slots at key airports have also made it more difficult for new airlines to enter the market. Airlines continue to demonstrate greater supply constraint than in the years following deregulation, but with the industry still somewhat fragmented, capacity restraint remains a challenge.

✱The lesson is that industries with low barriers to entry have a more difficult time achieving competitive equilibrium. Whenever OPEC has been successful at raising oil prices, higher returns have spurred production from non-OPEC producers, most recently by US shale drillers. Technology has lowered the entry barriers for brokerage and lending, putting pressure on commissions and lending margins despite industry consolidation. Whenever reinsurance rates tighten after some event, outside investors are quick to capitalize on excess returns, and the insurance sector remains highly competitive. The internet has lowered barriers to entry for authors, musicians, and products influenced by social media, impacting returns in publishing, music, clothing, and beauty segments.

Longer Asset Life Makes Learning More Painful

The quicker the feedback, the faster one can learn - true for companies as well as people. Companies, as do investors, make mistakes, and the quicker one can change course, the better. Consequently, industries where decisions play out quickly are more attractive than those that develop slowly. Airplanes last 30 years, and even if an airline goes out of business, the plane remains a functioning asset and excess supply takes years to absorb. Once an airline has opted for a certain fleet type, reversing that decision becomes more expensive. Aircraft manufacturers, Boeing and Airbus, battle for orders despite having a duopoly. On the other hand, the life of a rental car is less than two years, enabling supply/demand to get back in balance more quickly. Like planes, cruise ships last decades, but the useful life of a long-haul truck is about five years so in the absence of strong demand, truckers can more quickly bring supply into balance than cruise lines or hotels. In the oil sector, traditional wells last 20-30 years, but oil sourced from fracking has a much shorter life, which makes US supply much more variable than in the past. On the other hand, pipelines and refineries last decades, making midstream and downstream returns much more dependent on demand to fix imbalances.

Barriers to exit

Most investors pay attention to barriers to entry, but barriers to exit are equally important. Just as death is needed for life on earth to thrive, a good company cannot truly succeed if unsuccessful competitors are not permitted to fail. Equity investors should be wary of businesses with high barriers to exit. Common causes of high barriers to exit include nationalism, bankruptcy rules, and supplier dependence.

If a government believes an industry has national importance, then a local company in that sector will not be permitted to disappear, which will preserve uneconomic supply and consequently keep prices low for all industry participants. Almost every country feels that they need to have a national airline, regardless of their lack of competitiveness, and even the US government has repeatedly subsidized the airline industry during times of crisis. An investor is probably better off investing in debt rather than equity of companies viewed as nationally important. Governments have also stepped in to protect their auto sectors during economic downturns - often to protect jobs. Governments frequently use tariffs to protect local industries when prices fall, keeping alive auto as well as steel manufacturers and sometimes apparel producers.

In the United States, bankruptcy laws are pro-debtor. On the one hand, bankrupt companies can be restructured to become more efficient competitors, but bankruptcy often keeps zombie companies alive, keeping prices artificially low for competitors and indirectly causing other companies in the sector to file for bankruptcy. Airlines are once again a poster child for these negative industry dynamics. For airlines, the bankruptcy process can last years and some airlines have undergone several bankruptcies, keeping an uneconomic supply operating continuously.

Suppliers (labor and customers) can also create high barriers to exit, particularly when supplier margins are higher than their customers. Unionized workers often step in to save faltering companies rather than risk losing their seniority benefits and relatively higher pay/benefits. In airlines, autos, steel, and trucks, workers have offered concessions to keep their companies alive. It is also not only unionized workers that keep excess supply in place. For example, Wall Street has anticipated a shakeout of equity research capacity for decades. Despite the disappearance of many mid-sized investment banks, new research boutiques have sprung up as unemployed analysts discover that even after a pay cut, the boutiques offer better compensation than other professions. During bankruptcies, the aircraft and engine manufacturers often sided with management over other creditors. By keeping airlines flying, the engine manufacturers continued to enjoy the maintenance revenue streams generated by usage, and the aircraft manufacturers took actions to preserve their loyal customers. Bankruptcies typically occur during economic downturns, and aircraft lessors tend to be lenient to their airline customers because during a recession, the lessor has few other customers for the plane. More recently, shopping malls stepped in to aid their retail customers during COVID because the malls had few other options for renting out their space.

Finding a Business with a Sustainable Edge

For most analysts, the initial approach to a company is to consider what could go wrong. One of my favorite clients, Ken Heebner of Capital Growth, was one of the few portfolio managers who regularly asked, *"What could go right?"* With that positive attitude in mind, let us examine what characteristics can provide a business with a sustainable edge. I have organized them into the following categories: economies of scale, customer loyalty, flexibility, regulatory, and customer health.

Economies of Scale Come in Many Forms

Economies of scale offer the most common sustainable edge for a business and affect both the cost and revenue side of the equation. With the cost of a new semiconductor facility running in the billions of dollars, high barriers preclude new competition, and the expertise provided from years of research (R&D) have even prevented deep-pocketed Chinese competitors from penetrating the oligopoly. Makers of semiconductor equipment hold a similar advantage.

Production economies of scale can also be found in the chemical, packaging refining, smelting and utility sectors. Even in service businesses, such as exchanges and payments, unit costs benefit from the economies of scale. In agriculture, economies of scale are more significant in the processing end (grain, meatpackers) than the production end (farmers, cattle ranchers); consequently, agricultural production is far more fragmented than agricultural processing. A similar phenomenon is occurring in the nascent cannabis industry. Cost economies of scale appear less important in homebuilding, lending, and investment banking.

Hub and spokes systems create economies of scale. Larger airlines have generally outlasted smaller point-to-point carriers despite paying higher wages because their networks allow them to serve more markets with fewer assets and spread their infrastructure costs over more flights. Network economics help UPS and Fedex dominate package delivery and has enabled Amazon to start making its own inroads in the delivery business. The number of long-haul truckload shippers runs in the millions, but the top handful of less-than-truckload carriers, which enjoy economies of scale by aggregating shipments, control 75% of the market. However, larger size also introduces greater complexity, which can offset some of the cost benefits of economies of scale.

As Tesla discovered, the ability to mass-produce vehicles is a separate skill from engineering, and even the new electric vehicle companies are seeking to partner with the larger Original Equipment Manufacturers (OEMs), who have achieved economies of scale. Suppliers to the OEMs have also created engineering economies of scale due to their R&D efforts. Cummins has maintained a dominant share of the truck engine market despite manufacturers of commercial vehicles attempting to bring the work in-house owing to the complexity of meeting constantly changing emission requirements. Auto OEMs still rely on Borg Warner for engines and Aptiv for electronics because of their specialized knowledge, and energy exploration companies depend on the engineering expertise of Halliburton and Schlumberger.

Economies of scale generate purchasing power. The largest airlines typically can buy and finance planes much cheaper than their smaller competitors. Dicks Sporting Goods and Foot Locker receive a higher allocation of hotter-selling items as well as secure lower prices than the independent stores. Department stores, groceries and pharmacies may enjoy a similar edge. The US government turned to CVS and Walgreens to distribute COVID-19 vaccines owing to their extensive distribution. Hotel and restaurant franchisers benefit from economies of scale for advertising, loyalty programs and supplies, which they pass along to their franchises in return for a fee. Visa and Mastercard earn their fees by offering card-issuing banks near universal access to merchants.

Economies of scale in distribution, assisted by a low cost of capital, can often overcome a lack of innovation. Despite their larger R&D budgets, the largest tech companies (Facebook, Google, and Microsoft) have not developed many significant new products, but have created shareholder value by purchasing start-up technology as well as potential competitors and plugging these products into their strong distribution networks. Similarly, large pharmaceutical corporations often receive better returns by purchasing developmental drugs discovered by smaller biotech companies than from their own R&D spend. In life science, acquisitions have enabled

Thermo Fisher to capitalize on its access to academia, government hospitals, labs, and pharma, and Stryker has successfully expanded its product line in medical devices by purchasing smaller competitors.

Economies of scale are the principal driver of Roll-ups, a strategy of buying and combining smaller businesses. This strategy has shown to be effective in a diverse range of sectors: dealerships (auto/truck), doctor/dental practices, equipment rental, financial/insurance advisory, and industrial distribution. Equity markets often award roll-up stocks higher multiples than other companies in the sector, providing an extra incentive to the acquirer by making the acquisition immediately accretive.

Economies of scale can make a company smarter. In today's world of artificial intelligence, more transactions translate into more data and better decisions. The tech world calls this "The Flywheel Effect" and is most prominent in Search, which Google dominates through its ability to anticipate your information request with just a few keystrokes. By following your movements on the web, internet advertising can help merchants more efficiently target their efforts, a practice made harder by Apple's recent opt-out policies. Insurance companies have years of data via customer experience (including data generated over the years from customers via tracking devices) that insurtech start-ups will find difficult to replicate. Fintechs hope to use customer information available on the web to better gauge the risk of default and improve over time. For autonomous driving, more vehicles on the road will result in faster learning and safer systems for the early winners.

Technology can sometimes subvert economies of scale. Amazon has replaced department stores as a one-stop shopping experience and sites like Carvana may offer better used car availability than dealers. While prominence in store display is still an important advantage for large beauty and household product companies, the shift to virtual shopping has made prominence in internet search display equally important. In addition, social media can level the playing field for smaller companies that are competing against the huge advertising dollars of their larger rivals. The combination of streaming voice over internet and wireless technology replaced landline phone service's consumer monopoly. Streaming has also upended the business of cable operators, which previously controlled what viewers could see. Wireless service is dominated by three providers (Verizon, AT&T, and TMobile-Sprint), which brag about their nationwide coverage (another term for economies of scale), but cable companies are hoping that by pooling the power of all of their Wi-Fi connections, they can compete in the wireless communications business at much lower cost.

Customer Loyalty

Good businesses have loyal customers - even if it is against their will. Investors should look for businesses that have proprietary service or products that customers find unique. Products and services with high switching costs also create customer stickiness as can those tied to specific locations.

Data is viewed as increasingly valuable to companies, particularly financials, and companies that sell proprietary data are often awarded higher multiples. Gartner and Verisk Analytics standout in this regard, but Dun & Bradstreet, FactSet and Thomson Reuters also have unique data sets. Software providers can provide unique services - sometimes by offering a product customizable to a specific industry (Guidewire for property insurance) and sometimes a product that is easily customizable - i.e., Shopify for ecommerce payment/shipping, Bill.com for back office, and Wix.com for website development. Besides complexity and depth of industry knowledge, successful software companies offer easy to use, scalable and reliable operating systems and continually introduce new products as well as update/upgrade existing ones.

Branding is about turning seemingly commoditized goods into unique products and usually there is substance behind the premium image. My household will only use Tide detergent, and both Starbucks and Dunkin Donuts have loyal followings among coffee drinkers based on taste differences. McDonald's fries drive traffic as much as their burgers, and most consumers can tell the difference between a chocolate cookie sandwich with vanilla creme and an Oreo. Sporting goods companies differentiate their products on performance - Nike enables athletes to run faster and jump higher and Calloway helps golfers hit the ball farther and straighter. We'll never be as good as LeBron James or Tiger Woods, but we can at least dream and us amateurs need all the help we can get. The Ferrari and Tesla brands may be carefully cultivated, but they have strong engineering backing their images. Movie companies with film franchises (James Bond, Star Wars, Harry Potter, and Marvel) have far more reliable revenue streams than production companies based on stand-alone movies. Even industrial companies have brands - Monsanto and DuPont turned seeds into unique products with particular attributes.

One way to determine customer stickiness among suppliers is to determine if the company is an order maker or order taker. Order makers win business based on product features and earn higher margins than order takers, which tend to win on price or execution. In technology, I would consider Corning an order maker because its LCD glass for flat panel display has special properties, but would consider even the efficient electronic contract manufacturers (Celestica, Flex, Jabil, Sanmina) and IT distributors (Synnex, Arrow Electronics) order takers since their customers control their most proprietary technology. In autos, engine efficiency and electronic suppliers are order makers while suppliers of auto bodies, interiors and tires are order takers. Despite their duopoly, aircraft manufacturers Airbus and Boeing have lower margins than many of their suppliers, whose technology the OEMs cannot replicate. New aircraft designs generally follow breakthroughs in engine design rather than aircraft aerodynamics so aircraft engine suppliers are order makers.

Customer service can build loyalty; Chewy has been able to successfully compete against Amazon by offering a more personalized relationship with pet owners. Airline service is relatively undifferentiated, but airlines have created loyalty through frequent flier programs. Concentrating your service with one carrier gives you higher status (more upgrades) and enables you to more quickly earn enough miles (typically for business, commanding a higher fare) to obtain a free trip (usually for leisure, replacing what is normally a lower fare). Switching airlines would force the miles-hungry consumer to start from scratch.

Companies can keep customers wedded to their product by thoroughly integrating them into our personal and work lives. Salesforce.com and Microsoft have so infiltrated corporate IT systems that switching costs to another provider would be time-consuming and expensive. Once a consumer is firmly entrenched in Apple's ecosystem (iPhone, iTunes, iMac, iWatch and a host of other apps), the disadvantages of leaving the system start to outweigh the higher cost. Longer learning curves contribute to stickiness. Hospitals and labs are reluctant to switch diagnostic and medical equipment given the costs and risks from doctors and lab workers having to adapt to new technologies. Southwest Airlines has remained a loyal Boeing customer for years because of the benefit of operating a single fleet of planes, which not only helps minimize capital invested in parts inventory but also reduces training time for maintenance and flight crew.

Being the in Right Place at the Right Time

It is said, "*there are three things that matter in property: location, location and location.*" Two buildings may be identical, but a building in New York City is worth more than one in Buffalo. Real estate isn't the only business where location matters. Streaming may threaten cable programming, but the customer still needs the internet connection the cable company provides. as compared to wireless service, which is easier to switch. A competitor can run the same truck route as a competitor, but railroad tracks are difficult to replicate. Trucks can compete against rails for some goods, but generally, railroads are more efficient carrying larger quantities of heavier goods and containers longer distances.

The location offers protection for other industries that carry heavier cargo and certain services. Aggregates and sand (for drilling) are expensive to transport, limiting the number of competitors beyond a certain distance from the buyer. Competition in waste management is also very local. Consequently, aggregate miners like Vulcan Materials and Martin Marietta boast higher margins and less price volatility than other miners. Waste Management and Republic Services have also proven to be less cyclical than other industrial companies. Location can also matter for data centers (lower latency) and hospitals (longer travel times endanger the patient).

The travel sector also demonstrates the importance of location specificity. If one wants to fly to Atlanta, or Dallas or Houston, the choice of carriers is limited, giving the hub airline pricing power, particularly if choosing the most popular departure times. However, if one wants to rent a car in any of these airports at any time, one has a plethora of choices and prices tend to be very competitive (except in these post-COVID times when all rental car companies are short vehicles). One's choice of hotels is also greater except where location within a city is important. On the other hand, if a traveler flies to a non-hub city, the number of connecting opportunities tends to be broader and pricing more competitive.

Good Businesses are Less Dependent on Factors beyond their Control

An investor should always be wary of businesses that have factors out of their control. Given the difficulty of predicting mother nature, weather-dependent companies are hard to forecast. Consequently, the market tends to award low multiples to many agricultural-related businesses. Companies tied to lawn care are subject to overly wet or cool springs, and apparel makers and vendors can suffer when the winter is not cold enough or the spring is too short. Businesses tied to winter conditions could be particularly challenged with global warming - shorter, warmer winters could hurt demand for ski resorts, winter sports equipment or even road salt.

Markets tend to be skeptical of companies tied to fashion or consumer fads, which have unpredictable cycles. In these sectors, investors should favor companies that have shorter lead times. Spanish retailer Zara has always stood out for its *"read and react"* strategy, which monitors consumer data to accelerate production of hot-selling goods and curbing production of apparel that is becoming out of favor.

Nearly all businesses are dependent on the economy, which is out of a company's control. When the market fears a recession, multiples expand for less-economically sensitive stocks, such as utilities or defense corporations. For businesses with more cyclical demand, investors should prefer companies with a greater mix of aftermarket versus original equipment, rental versus purchase, shorter production/demand cycles, and a larger percentage of variable costs versus fixed costs.

Markets Value Consistency

In general, revenues from the aftermarket tend to be less volatile and higher margin than selling original equipment. In the automotive sector, companies selling aftermarket parts (Advance Auto Parts, Autozone, O'Reilly Automotive) and aftermarket services (Driven Brands, Mister Car Wash carry higher margins and multiples than auto manufacturers (Ford, GM) or suppliers (Magma). Makers of aircraft engines, electronics and breaks (i.e., General Electric, Rolls, Raytheon Technology) generate higher and more consistent margins than the aircraft manufacturers (Boeing and Airbus), and even within the former UTX, Otis elevators boasted better and steadier margins than Carrier, its refrigeration unit which had a much lower aftermarket mix. In the life science and medical device sectors, companies with a high percentage of sales from consumables out-earn those reliant purely on selling equipment. For tech, the shift from computing on-premise to the cloud has transformed a business largely selling hardware to one selling three times more software to help service customers operating in the cloud.

Markets prefer companies with more recurring revenue streams. In a way, technology has transformed from a business selling products to renting services. Rather than buy a license for a product that can quickly go obsolete, tech consumers now pay a monthly subscription fee for a product that is continually updated and upgraded, which creates a stickier relationship. Prior to COVID-19, gyms and other membership businesses also boasted attractive multiples. Many Planet Fitness members use their gyms sporadically, and by charging only $10-$20 a month, Planet Fitness is more likely to keep those aspirational customers than if they charged $200 annually and the lower usage enables Planet Fitness to serve more members per location. Franchising, in general, creates steadier, more attractive revenue streams than owning hotels or restaurants and contributes to Marriott's and McDonald's higher multiple versus peers.

For businesses that cannot control the volatility, look for companies that can adjust more quickly to demand swings. Airlines publish their schedules six months in advance so have little flexibility to match supply to short-term changes in demand. Because their assets last 30 years, excess supply can take years to absorb. In contrast, truckers can make more timely schedule adjustments, and because wear-and-tear leads to one-sixth of the truck fleet turning over each year, supply and demand can more quickly get back in balance. In a similar fashion, rental cars can bring supply and demand in balance more quickly than hotels and cruises.

Businesses with variable cost structures and shorter liability cycles can adapt faster to changes in revenue. In steel, blast furnaces operated by legacy producers like US Steel have higher fixed costs than Nucor, which uses electric arc furnaces to melt scrap steel. Asset-like home builders that buy finished lots, such as NVR, generate a higher return on assets and less volatile earnings than home builders that develop their own land. The semiconductor industry has improved profitability by moving to fabless manufacturing, in which they outsource their foundry operations.

Auto insurers like Progressive are better businesses than property and casualty insurers like AIG because their liabilities are more frequent but much more predictable in scope. HMOs are better businesses than long-term care where liabilities have a longer tail risk. Financials tied to payment processing have generated more consistent returns than companies tied to credit.

Regulation Generally Favors Larger Companies

Regulation carries a negative connotation for business, but can create barriers to entry, thereby protecting existing businesses. National security predominantly directs defense dollars to US companies. FAA approval for aircraft parts is an expensive and time-consuming process, but once incorporated in an aircraft design, provides a decades-long revenue stream. The Securities Exchange Commission requires bond ratings for many investment vehicles, which has created a profitable oligopoly for S&P,

Moody's and Fitch. Government housing guarantees led to the creation of companies dedicated to packaging loans to sell to government agencies, such as Fannie and Ginnie Mae. State regulations requiring home buyers seeking a mortgage to purchase title insurance - even when refinancing an existing home - generate strong cash flows for Fidelity National Finance.

Changes in regulation can lead to new business opportunities. Cummins has kept ahead of truck manufacturers in satisfying the periodic changes in emission requirements for trucks in the US, Europe, and rest of world. Most recently, air conditioning companies like Trane and Carrier have benefited from regulations requiring enhanced air filtration as a result of COVID-19. Dodd-Frank legislation was designed to reduce bank concentration by increasing the cost of capital for large banks, but by making the big banks appear safer to consumers, deposits are now even more concentrated in the largest banks.

On the other hand, governments operate under a slower timeframe than markets, and stocks involved in legislation, lawsuits and investigations can suffer long periods of stagnation. I'd be wary of businesses, such as cannabis and online gaming, which require changes in legislation to expand. The Chinese government has the power to make or break companies, and I'd avoid any stock that draws the attention of the Chinese government. Lawsuits tied to environmental and health issues can drag sectors down for decades as occurred for asbestos, cigarettes, lead, and opioids. More recently, PFAS (polyfluoroalkyl substances in products that may have adverse health effects), Roundup weedkiller, and baby powder are creating overhangs for 3M, Bayer, and Johnsons & Johnson, respectively.

Good Businesses have Healthy Customers

Lastly, steadier businesses tend to have healthier customers. Companies tied to federal, state and municipal government spending, such as defense stocks or waste, tend to be more resilient, albeit slower growing. Defense stocks have been particularly strong performers in periods of weaker economic growth because government pockets are so deep and neither political party wants to appear weak on national security. Furthermore, because military personnel overseeing the defense spending often end up working for defense companies, an incentive to push for accountability appears lacking, and defense industry margins have steadily climbed over the past few decades.

Just as consumer incomes are less volatile than corporate profits, businesses tied to less discretionary consumer spending are more defensive than those tied to corporate spending, which includes technology. COVID-19 distorted spending patterns in the 2020 recession, but I expect investors to be surprised by how much some areas of technology spending gets hit in the next recession, particularly Internet and tech firms serving smaller businesses, which tend to have shorter lifespans, or software products with long implementation lead times. Suppliers serving healthier customers tend to have higher margins. Just as the Aerospace & Defense Primes have higher margins than Automotive OEMs, suppliers to aerospace/defense boast higher returns than automotive suppliers. A-Mall REITs renting to bigger chains tend to outperform their B-Mall and strip mall peers. Even regulated utilities in higher-income states are able to raise rates more easily to invest in renewables and green technology.

A particularly attractive demographic are pets, which received a boost during the pandemic. Perhaps because gratitude is in short supply, people like to spoil their pets and may even spend more on their pets' health care than their own. The market awards a higher multiple to companies serving companion animals than livestock. Stocks heavily involved with pet care include Zoetis, Elanco, IDEXX Labs, Freshpet, and Chewy.

Good Management can Make a Difference

Good managers find a way to win and bad ones a way to lose, but distinguishing luck from skill is more art than science. Does the World Champion baseball team have the best manager or the best team? I think highly of Richard Anderson, the former CEO of Northwest Airlines and subsequently Delta, but he looked a lot smarter after his company merged with the more customer-friendly Delta labor groups. Similarly, investors viewed Continental Airlines management team less favorably after the company merged with the pricklier United employee unions.

For companies in which capital allocation is a critical skill, management quality is particularly important. Look at the track record of managers in acquisitions, whether the company has had the foresight to keep capital spending above peers in bad times and below peers in good times, and be wary of companies that seem to repurchase shares near market highs and issue shares near market lows. Bank of America's analyst Josh Shanker monitors whether insurers take on more risk at the peak or trough of cycles, favoring companies that take on more risk as prices rise and less risk as prices fall. I sometimes rely on the cringe factor. If a news item on a company crosses the tape and my first reaction is to cringe, then this is a sign of a management team that I should try to avoid.

Cycles Come in Many Forms

Long-term investors don't try to time cycles, except to capitalize on opportunities to buy high-quality companies that are undervalued owing to economic concerns. Nevertheless, guessing cycles correctly can lead to outsized returns, but the investor needs to know not only when to buy, but when to sell. Cycles do not only pertain to the overall economy but there are distinct cycles for autos, commodities, defense, housing, inventories, pricing, products and even stocks themselves have a life cycle. Understanding cycles is important even for non-cyclical stocks - consumer staples, defense, and utilities tend to underperform the market during periods of strong economic growth.

Of course, the stock market itself is one of the best leading indicators of economic growth, but that doesn't help investors who want to be a step ahead. Cyclical bull markets typically move in two phases - an anticipatory phase and an earnings-driven phase. On average, cyclical stocks start to climb three or four quarters ahead of the turning point in demand. Counterintuitively, around the time of the turning point, cyclical stocks often stage a brief correction as investors fret that the stocks have discounted too fast of a recovery. The second stage of a cyclical market is tied to the magnitude and duration of the earnings recovery. Perhaps because equity investors are an optimistic lot, the lead time for a bull market is much longer than a bear market. Cyclical bear stocks tend to have shorter lead times, but react more violently to bad news.

Look at the Haves, not the Have-nots

The consumer drives two-thirds of US GDP, so predicting consumer behavior is key to cyclical investing. Early in my career, Goldman Sachs top-rated retail analyst Joe Ellis argued that if you want to predict consumer spending, don't look at changes in the 5% who are unemployed but for the 95% who do have jobs. When wage growth outpaces inflation, consumer spending power rises, setting the stage for an economic upturn. Real wage growth has preceded an economic recovery in 5 of the last 6 cycles. During the 2020 pandemic, wage growth climbed 4%-5% with minimal inflation, which has contributed to the strong rebound in 2021. However, despite continued wage gains, inflation has outpaced wage growth in 2021, putting the recovery at risk if inflation doesn't moderate.

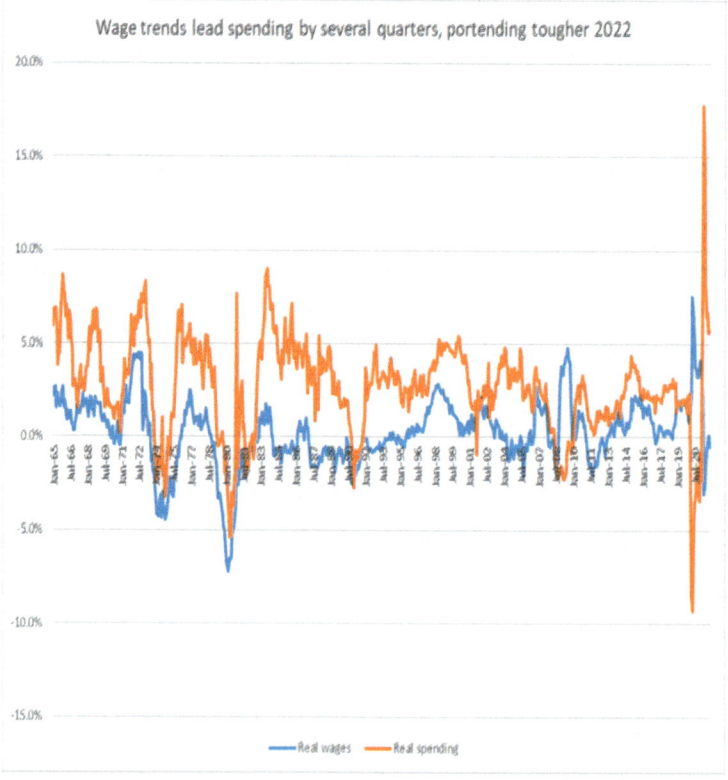

For corporations, the most reliable indicator for turning points in demand is the ISM manufacturing purchasing manager survey, which is surprisingly more useful than the ISM service index even though manufacturing represents a smaller percentage of the economy.

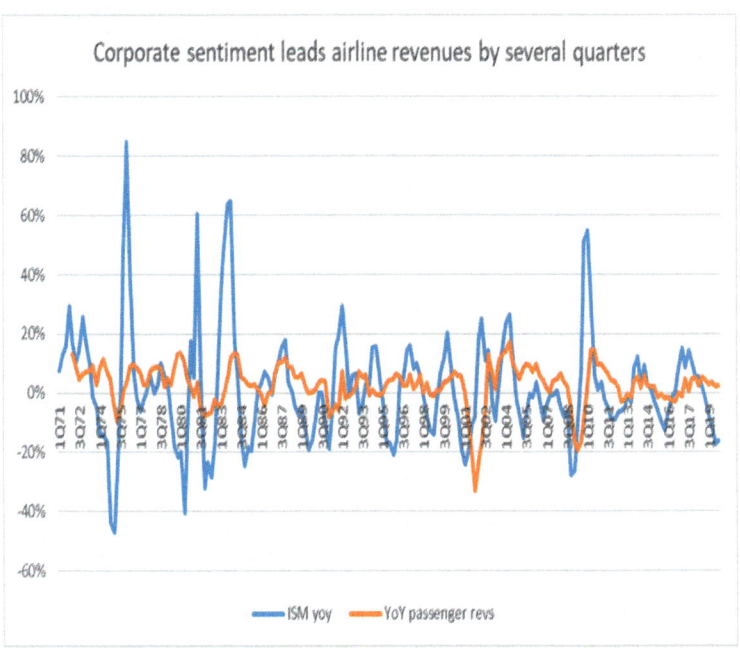

Another timely but more expensive set of data to track the economy is provided by ARC Corp., which clears booking transactions between airlines and travel agencies. Bookings lead travel by weeks and even months, so any indication of a pickup in corporate or leisure demand will quickly show up in ARC's data, which comes out with less than a week's delay. Since travelers tend to book their airline tickets before they book their hotel or rental car, airline bookings are also helpful leading indicators for lodging and rental car stocks. For surveys to be useful, the data must encompass at least one complete cycle. Nowadays, nearly all goods come in a box and travel by trucks. BofA's top-rated Paper & Packaging analyst George Staphos has been surveying box demand for 20 years, and BofA's highly-ranked Transportation analyst Ken Hoexter has been tracking trucking demand for nearly 15 years. I recommend both surveys as a way to gauge economic growth faster than the government statistics.

As mentioned previously, businesses benefit from a healthier customer base. Consequently, revenue acceleration is often preceded by improvements in customer economics. Unfortunately, for the investor, that lead time is fairly short. Stock prices of agricultural machinery, such as Caterpillar, Deere, and CNH Industrial, tend to quickly follow crop prices (corn, wheat, soy), which directly affect farmer incomes.

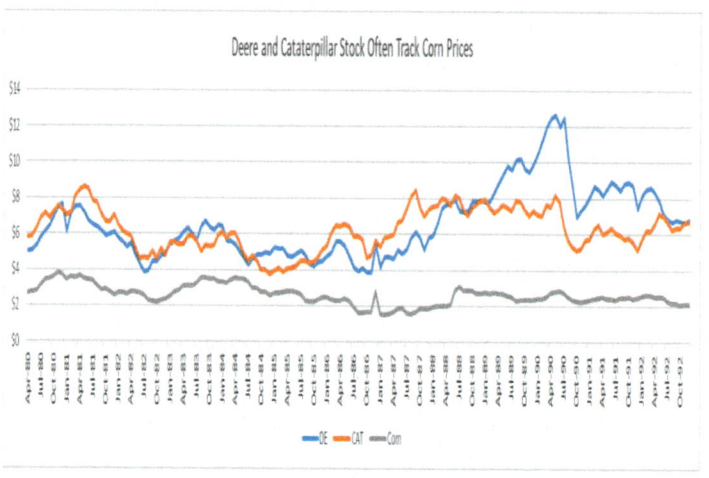

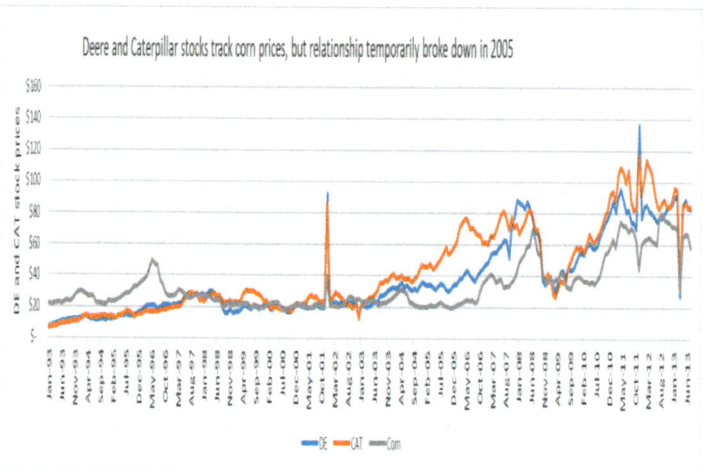

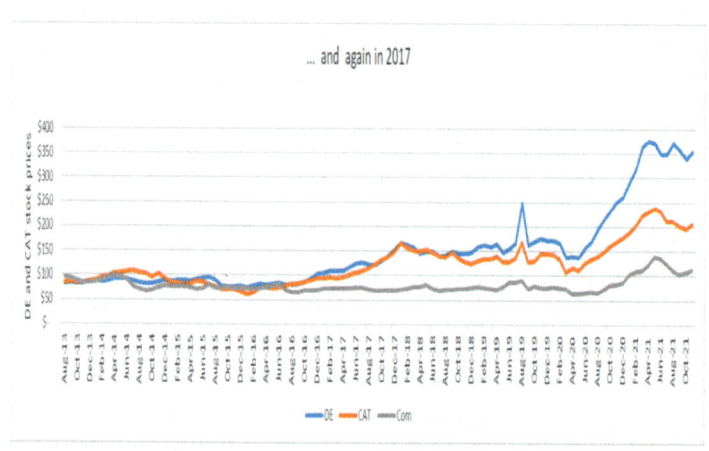

For oil service and energy production companies, the lead time between oil prices and stock prices is even shorter. On the other hand, a longer lag exists between an upturn in airline demand and plane deliveries given protracted production cycles.

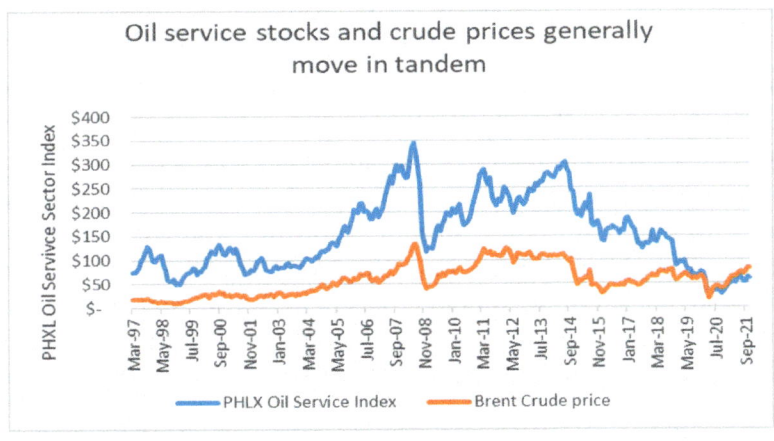

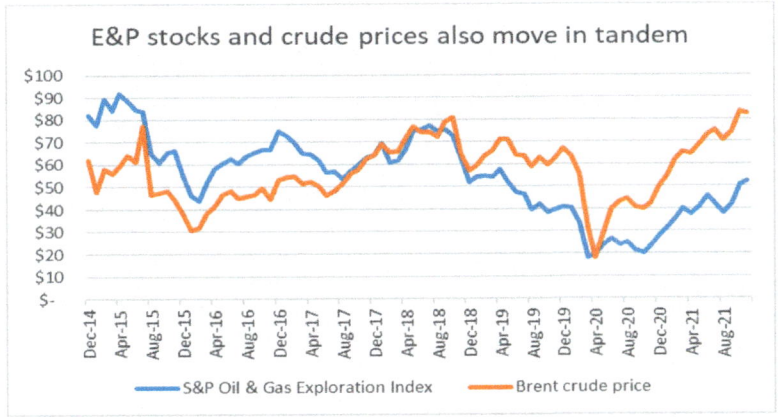

Sometimes, you need to be creative to find leading indicators. On the premise that business jets rely on an elite customer base, I found that the best way to predict demand for business jets (largest manufacturers being Bombardier, Dassault, Embraer, General Dynamics, Textron) was to monitor the number of billionaires on Forbes annual list of the world's richest people. Advisors shift money to asset managers with strong three and five-year track records. Asset managers with strong two-year track records or who are lapsing a period of bad performance can be good candidates for investors seeking turnaround stories in asset gathering. For automotive, an acceleration in miles driven typically precedes an improvement in auto maintenance, which is positive for engine lubricants (Valvoline, Energizer's STP), automotive paint (Axalta, AkzoNobel, PPG), and auto parts retailers but negative for auto insurers who see their claims rise.

Affordability can Presage Demand

Improved affordability presages better customer economics and higher sales. Since nearly all homes are mortgages, lower rates mean lower monthly payments. Even though housing prices consistently rose after the Great Financial Crisis, average monthly mortgage payments steadily declined through 2019 and despite shortages caused by a surge in pandemic-related demand, housing affordability is still better than a decade ago. Higher housing prices indirectly benefit housing-related demand by providing owners more equity to upgrade to bigger homes and/or refurbish existing homes, providing a lift to stocks like Home Depot and Lowes.

In a similar fashion, BofA Global Research monitors the monthly cost of owning and operating a car, and according to automotive analyst John Murphy, the real cost of owning a new car dropped 10% in 2020 and is now in line with post-Great Financial Crisis lows despite higher new car sticker prices. The biggest contributors to affordability are higher used car prices, which result in lower implied depreciation rates, lower interest costs, and better trade-in values. Consequently, auto demand surprised to the upside in 2021 despite production constraints.

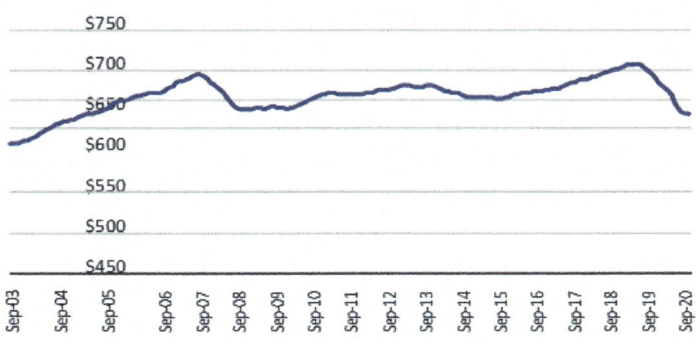

Source: BofA Global Research

I believe the importance of affordability is particularly underappreciated relative to aircraft demand. As with houses, airlines finance most aircraft over a 25-year period via debt or lease. Using a mortgage calculator, one can convert the price of a new plane into a monthly payment. Despite new plane prices having more than doubled over the past 40 years, the monthly lease rate of a plane over the past forty years has barely budged thanks to the sharp drop in interest rates. When inflation-adjusted, the monthly cost is nearly 70% lower. The affordability of aircraft is even more pronounced for non-US buyers. Given the decline in the value of the dollar, the nominal monthly lease payment for a Chinese airline in renminbi or Japanese airline in yen is 20% lower than in 1980. Consistent with affordability, demand for aircraft for non-US buyers has outpaced that of US airlines.

Inventory and Credit Cycles Magnify Momentum

Swings in inventory and availability of credit can create mini-cycles of their own, but often magnify existing trends, accelerating downward trends at the start of a recession and hastening the upwards trends at the start of a recovery. Most companies measure inventory in terms of days' supply - the amount of inventory divided by daily demand. Consequently, when demand falters, not only does the company have to reduce production to meet a lower level of demand, but must also bring down the level of inventories, which no longer need to be as high. Production then falls faster than demand, resulting in lower hourly wages, which leads to a decline in overall consumer spending, and ultimately need for further production cuts. Conversely, once demand has stabilized, production no longer has to be less than demand and can start to rise to meet the new equilibrium level, requiring more man-hours and creating a positive feedback loop for the economy or at the very least, ending the negative feedback loop. Even fears of shortages can create an inventory cycle. During the pandemic, concern about the supply of toilet paper and cleaning supply led to a surge in hoarding, which could cause a hangover for these producers in 2021. Currently, chip shortages may be creating a similar phenomenon though the chip shortages themselves are forcing auto manufacturers to curtail production, which will shift auto supply and, therefore chip demand into 2022 or 2023.

Housing isn't the only Industry with Credit Cycles

Credit cycles aren't only about rates, but about the availability of credit, too. The decline in rates certainly contributed to the 2006-2008 housing bubble, but the lack of credit discipline was a greater factor. People could purchase homes with no down payment, lengthy deferrals on principal repayment, little income to support the loan, and virtually no documentation. The stock market bubble in the 1920s was similarly boosted by the ability for speculators to buy on margin, and the recent surge in retail trading arising from ease of access to margin accounts via online brokers has contributed to the volatility in certain meme stocks.

The experiences of Boeing versus Textron in the Great Financial Crisis demonstrate the importance of credit in creating winners and losers. Both companies possessed huge aircraft backlogs going into the crisis, yet Boeing's backlog proved firm and Textron's illusive. For commercial aircraft, airlines typically finance planes through public, private and government-private secured financings. Even though most airlines suffered huge losses, government-based export-import banks provided a financing bridge during 2008-2009 and the aircraft manufacturers like Boeing were able to continue to sell planes throughout the recession. In contrast, even though the customers for business jets were wealthy, the market for financing business jets was generally closed during this timeframe. Cessna's business jet sales plummeted more than 60% from 2008 to 2010 and did not start to recover until 2014.

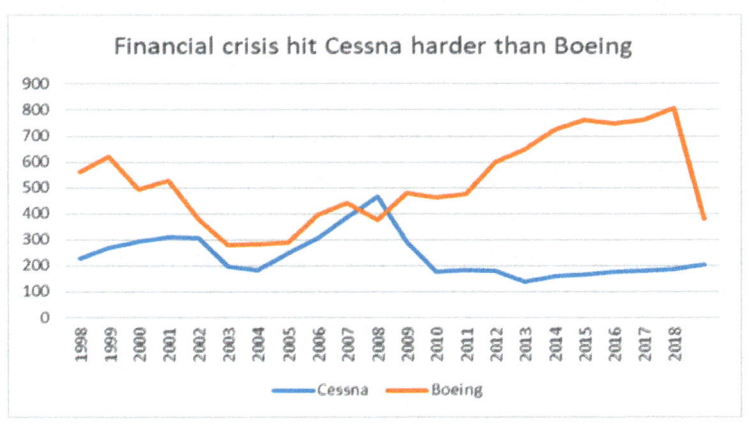

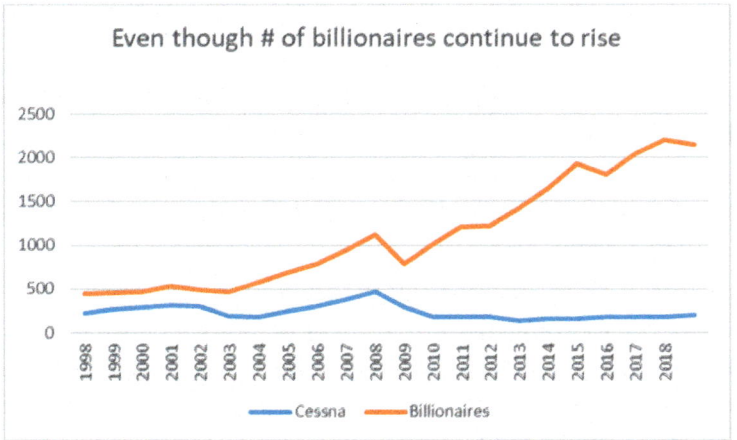

Differentiated access to credit shaped the post-crisis economic recovery as well. Dodd-Frank was designed to improve financial stability and consumer protection, and banks are certainly healthier today than ever before. By requiring a greater capital buffer for riskier loans, the law provides incentives to banks to avoid speculative credits. In practice, this has led to banks to increase their share of lending to higher quality credits such as large companies and wealthy individuals and reduce their share of lending to smaller companies and the middle class, thereby contributing to the growing wealth gap between the rich and everyone else. The Great Financial Crisis also highlighted the importance of duration risk - the matching of cash inflows and outflows. Companies like General Electric that overly relied on short-term debt have never fully recovered from the 2008 liquidity crunch, which ended sinking investment banks, Lehman and Bear Stearns. More recently, credit dislocations in the spring of 2020 clobbered Mortgage REITs, which generally finance their long-term assets with short-term debt.

Product Cycles

The market treats product cycles a bit like economic cycles in that stocks move in anticipation of the cycle, correct around the time the product is introduced and then the final leg depends on the magnitude of the product's sales. Because human beings tend to be overly optimistic, initial sales often lag estimates. Biotech investors call this *"sell the launch."* Often the biggest move in biotech stocks is the period prior to an including the approval of the drug, and even for successful drugs, the sales ramp can take longer than expected. The introduction of new products is a catalyst for growth in tech, communications, consumer gadgets, entertainment, retail and even vehicles. In some industries, such as aircraft and mobile phones, new products can lead to a lull in sales prior to the launch. On the other hand, new products necessitated by regulation can lead to a final surge in buying for the existing product, as occurs for new trucks that are often more expensive and less fuel-efficient than their predecessor because of stricter emission rules.

The stocks of Film studios like Disney often move ahead of major blockbuster releases, which are scheduled years in advance. Products tied to movies (Hasbro and Mattel for toys, Funko for collectables) see their fortunes swing with box office successes. Fashion cycles can drive apparel and retail. The popularity of athleisure has shifted share in the past decade, but changes in fashion trends appear less pronounced than the past. Emphasizing the importance of new models to drive market share, Bank of America's John Murphy puts out a product called Car Wars, which quantifies the degree to which each auto manufacturer refreshes its product portfolio.

Supply Cycles more Predictable than Demand Cycles

Thus far, I have concentrated on cycles in demand, which is less predictable than supply, but capacity cycles can overwhelm demand cycles in determining prices, particularly for commodities. In many industries, the process of adding new capacity requires long lead times. Companies tend to initiate expansion plans during good times, only to see that capacity put in place after demand has peaked. In a typical supply cycle, companies cut back supply during a downturn in recessions, which stabilizes prices as demand bottoms. As volumes recover, supply tightens, resulting in higher prices, but spurs companies to start expanding. In the mid-to-later part of the recovery, the growth in supply starts to match demand, causing prices to first flatten and then fall as volumes turn south. Airlines order planes years in advance, and price increases typically start to decelerate mid-cycle, even as demand remains firm. With shorter delivery timelines than planes, truck orders are usually a good inverse leading indicator for truck transportation pricing. In the insurance sector, supply also drives pricing. Perversely, insurance stocks often do well after catastrophes because large claims losses discourage new capital from coming into the market, setting the stage for a positive pricing cycle.

Among commodities, production comes on most slowly for mining, which bodes well for a prolonged bull market in copper, given supply will take several years to respond to the growth in demand as the economy becomes more electrified. For lumber and agricultural crops, production can be adjusted more quickly, creating shorter cycles. Traditional oil finds, particularly offshore, can take several years to reach production, but fracking now enables US companies to respond much more quickly and is likely to lead to shorter cycles with narrower oil price moves. Aluminum, chemicals, and steel plants take several years to build, and currently, the outlook for chemical and particularly steel supply looks to overtake demand in 2022-2023, leading to what BofA steel analyst Timna Tanners calls "*Steelmageddon.*" Capacity additions look very aggressive for lithium, but industries with faster underlying demand can more quickly absorb supply as compared to paper, which must continually contract to keep ahead of shrinking demand. Buildings like factories take several years to come to fruition. Currently, the expected supply growth in hotels, offices and apartments looks relatively tame overall, but overbuilding is occurring in certain major cities.

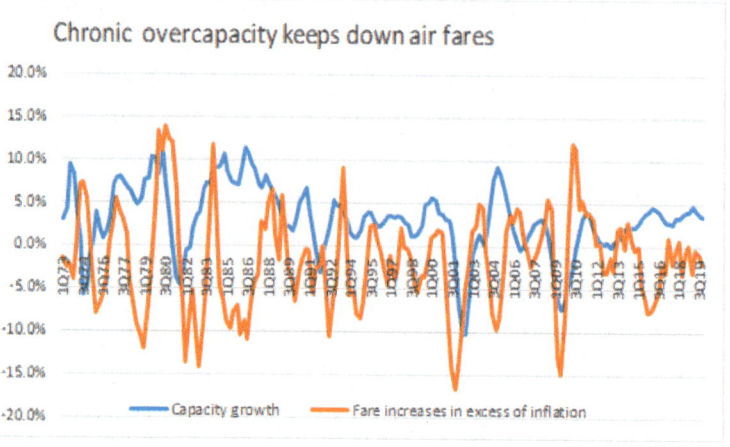

Source: Airlines for America.

Are Tech Stocks the New Consumer Staples?

Understanding cycles is even important for non-cyclical stocks. The multiples of Utilities, consumer staples and defense stocks expand during periods of economic uncertainty when consistency is rewarded, but these sectors underperform when the economy roars as occurred in 2021. Retail stocks outperform industrials when the sales-production gap is high and underperform industrials when production starts outpacing consumer spending. During the pandemic, tech stocks proved much more resilient than in past recessions. Some of the technology (video conferencing, remote desktops, remote security) is likely to be less resilient in the next recession, but Apple products, Amazon e-tail, and Google search are such an integral part of our lives, they have become just as much a consumer staple as Procter & Gamble. For businesses, managing data centers on Amazon and Microsoft may be the new staples, and tech companies are increasingly moving to the subscription model to become business staples. On the other hand, some tech spending can be postponed (i.e., adtech, development ops) and technology tied to industrial demand will remain cyclical.

Life Cycle of a Stock

Finally, ownership of a company's stock follows a life cycle of its own, which can create risks and opportunities - a concept I learned from Michael Karsch, former portfolio manager of Soros and Karsch Capital. New companies are typically owned by growth investors. As the company turns profitable and growth moderates, GARP (investors seeking growth at a reasonable price) step in. Eventually, growth stalls, multiples drop further and value investors step in. The process of changing the investor base creates dislocations, and the risk and opportunity are that stocks overshoot both on the upside and the downside along the way. Highly cyclical stocks frequently see a change in their shareholder base. During periods of losses, distressed investors are the primary buyers. When cash flows stabilize, value investors step in to buy the shares. As profits rise, some investors start believing that *"this time is different"* and the business will be less cyclical than in the past, at which time some GARP and momentum investors start to buy as well. More often than not, profits again plunge in the next recession, and the ownership cycle starts anew.

Spin-offs create opportunities for investors partly because the newly separated stock does not match the investing criteria of the existing shareholder base. Often the parent company will spin-off a company that is either non-core and/or has a different growth profile than the parent. The initial holders of the spin-off often sell their newly issued shares, putting pressure on the stocks as has occurred recently when utilities spin off their pipeline assets. However, not only can this dislocation cause a stock to be underpriced, but the spin-off tends to also benefit from the increased attention from a dedicated management team.

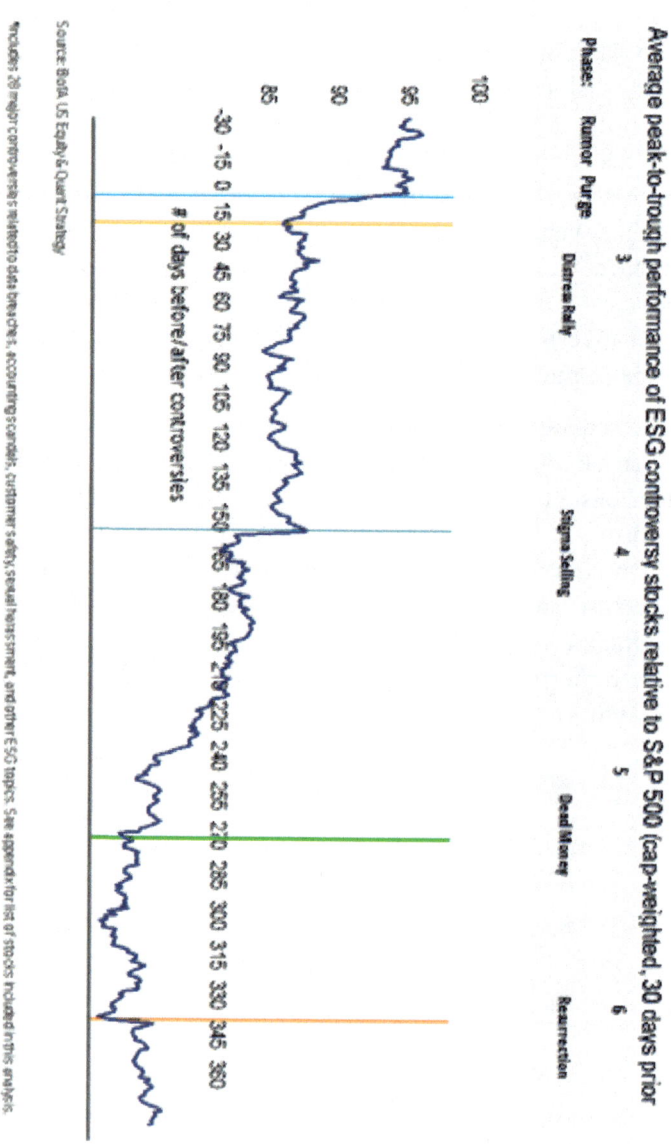

Savita Subramanian, an equity strategist at Bank of America Global Research, notes that stocks involved in controversies have their own lifecycle and investors should be wary of stepping in too early. Stocks involved in controversies often underperform in the weeks prior to the issue erupting as the warning signs start to trickle out and the market begins to anticipate problems. The drop in stock price in the weeks after the controversy becomes public is multiple times the magnitude of the anticipation decline. Stocks with high ESG ownership are often hit hardest by controversies, and the majority of ESG funds dump their positions within a few months. Around two months after the controversy, distressed buyers step in and drive a brief rally, but controversies usually involve deeply ingrained problems and controversy stocks on average bottom three months after the event and then stagnate until fixes are in place – only then do the stocks revive. The controversy cycle typically lasts nearly a year, but in the Volkswagen diesel emission scandal, VW stock did not meaningfully outperform the auto index until six years after the scandal.

Big Data

Most investors have access to economic data from the government, financial data from companies, and industry-specific data provided by industry trade groups or data vendors. Some industry data is free, such as railroad carloadings. However, much data costs money to access, giving hedge funds and mutual funds an edge over ordinary investors. As mentioned earlier in this book, the Airline Reporting Corp sells weekly travel agency booking data. IMS offers data on pharmacy transactions, which reveals brand-specific trends on various drug sales. Neilsen provides data on sales and volumes data generated by point-of-sales systems for 90 US retail chains as well as its better-known media information on what people are watching and streaming. In addition, hedge funds and large money managers are buying data using your credit cards, geolocation, and phone apps - a bit creepy even though the data is anonymized.

In this section, I will describe some of the sources of alternative data and provide use cases. In general, I have found alternative data more useful for traders than investors and categorize them in the following buckets: trending, mapping, regulatory, ESG (Environmental, Social and Governance), and analytic. Trending is data that seeks to capture changes in momentum. Mapping adds a geographic element to the trending data and use of regulatory data can help predict government actions. ESG is data designed to capture nonfinancial risk factors, and I define analytic as quantitative methods for analyzing the data itself.

Trending Data - Surveys, Internet, Social Media, and Credit Cards

As cited previously, surveys can provide a useful gauge of demand, particularly if sent out to targeted audiences, such as shippers, hospitals, purchasing managers or manufacturers. These surveys are not predictive but represent current demand, and the information can provide a faster read on trends than published data. In an attempt to be more predictive, analysts also survey spending intentions targeted to specific groups, such as Chief Technology Officers for tech spending or Corporate Travel Departments. Surveys can also be effective to predict drug adoption by doctors or software penetration for accountants, financial advisors or other specialized use cases. There are various software tools (i.e., SurveyMonkey) to create surveys that accurately reflect the population whose opinion the user wants to measure. Common surveys include purchase intentions for big-ticket items, such as cars, houses, and appliances. The frequency of surveys has recently increased to determine whether pandemic-related behavior changes are temporary or longer-lasting.

Surveys are also useful for gauging investor sentiment. A trader needs to know not only what will happen, but what is expected to happen. Often stocks fall after strong earnings because expectations were already built into the stock. Bank of America has surveyed global fund managers for nearly 30 years, and Chief Investment Strategist Michael Hartnett has formulated a fairly successful bull-bear indicator for contrarians. Stocks often bottom during periods of peak bearishness (high cash levels are one input) and peak during periods of peak bullishness. Survey also reveals consensus views on economic growth, inflation and favored sectors. More and more, analysts are using surveys to gauge investor opinions on individual stocks, but the sample set is not usually large and broad enough to be meaningful. On the other hand, services like Visible Alpha allow investors to see analyst estimates on a granular basis (in pharma even down to the individual drug level) to glean whether and where Wall Street's expectations are too optimistic or pessimistic.

Consumers who buy products typically search first on the web. Consequently, one of the simplest ways to gauge demand is to look at the number of search requests for a product using Google trends or Baidu if seeking Chinese input. Comparing the number of search requests in different brands of the same product (i.e., handbags) could also give you insights into market share changes and Google even provides this on a regional basis. Certain brands have strong ties to athletes and other celebrities so the rise and or fall in their popularity (number of Twitter followers, or searches on Google) could suggest changes in demand - such as Steph Curry for Under Armour sneakers, Tiger Woods and Lebron James for Nike, Kardashian/Jenner for beauty products, or Joe Rogen for Spotify.

Many companies offer help in analyzing customer engagement on the web - for example, Google, ComScore, StatCounter, Similarweb. Tracking the number of visits to a company website and the amount of time viewers spent on the site indicates the strength of the customer's relationship to the brand. The average user spends nearly 2.5 hours on social media, but the time spent on platforms appears to have peaked, particularly for Facebook, as younger people shift to newer entrants like TikTok. For gaming companies or online betting platforms, measuring the number of downloaded apps as well as customer engagement is a reliable way to track adoption.

Web scraping is a useful though a more time-consuming way of extracting data from the internet, although there are various companies (i.e., Blue Prism, Kofax, UiPath) that can automate the process. These services can keep track of thousands of prices for an item each day, but building a useful database can take months. For example, one could compare the prices of Walmart to various grocers (Albertson, Amazon Prime, Fresh Market, Kroger, Target), BestBuy prices to various other tech sellers, or competing chains Dollar General versus Dollar Tree and Family Dollar. A widening gap could indicate that shares will soon shift to the company offering the most competitive prices. Travel provides a good web scraping use case. Not only can you compare the prices of various hotel chains by city, but Shaun Kelley and Justin Post of BofA Global Research use data from AirDNA to track the number and prices of alternative accommodations listings like those provided by Airbnb and VRBO. Increasingly, these listings offer competition to hotel room rates and have curtailed the pricing power of hotel chains in some of the larger cities.

UBS Evidence Lab scrapes websites for insights into housing by monitoring the growth of listings, the length of time a house was listed before being sold, and sales prices relative to the existing asking price. Data collected on agency branches and agent counts can be used as inputs for estimates for realty brokerage stocks like RE/MAXX and Realogy, and price trackers for used cars and equipment can signal changes in trends in the markets for new cars and machinery. Finally, web scraping of online reviews could alert investors more quickly regarding changes in customer satisfaction for consumer and technology products.

Social media can be used to hop on quickly for sentiment swings. Twitter buzz can quickly capture whether a new movie is a hit or a dud. However, gauging sentiment is difficult since computers don't understand sarcasm and context can determine whether words are positive or negative. TickerTags analyzes social media buzz, signals users of changes in sentiment tied to a ticker, and would have cautioned investors away from buying Seaworld after the documentary Blackfish criticized their handling of orcas. In addition, TickerTags can alert users when new topics or keywords are associated with a stock. If the word e-coli or salmonella starts to trend in a restaurant stock's Twitter feed, that would obviously be a bad sign. BofA Global Research now monitors mentions of stocks or stock tickers on Reddit's WallStreetBets to predict which stocks are most vulnerable to volatility caused by retail investors swarming in and out of "*meme*" stocks.

Through services like Yodlee, hedge funds and other investors can purchase anonymized data that allows users to analyze spending trends from credit card, bank, investment, and travel reward accounts. BofA Global Economics Research has used anonymized data from its own 58 million card issuers to analyze spending patterns during the pandemic. Data revealed that spending declined sharply for high-income earnings during the pandemic but increased for low-income earnings owing to government stimulus, which suggests a post-pandemic recovery is likely to be led by high-income spending. Data also revealed how much spending share shifted from services to goods and from bricks and mortars to ecommerce. Spending on services is now rebounding sharply, but much of ecommerce gains look to be stickier. Within travel, lodging has recovered more quickly than airlines while cruises continue to underperform.

Mapping - Location, Phones, Satellites, Weather

AggData provides a list of store, factory, government and other location data, which can be easily visualized using Google's Tableau software. Location data enables one to see competitive store overlap. For example, within a 5 miles area, how many Dominos have a Pizza Hut, Papa John or Little Caesar competitor or how many McDonalds have a nearby Burger King or Wendy's? Which retailers benefited most when Aeropostale or Sears closed? Are new store openings targeted towards any particular retailer? When Home Depot decided to make Masco their primary paint choice for contractors, Bank of America's chemicals analyst Steve Byrne determined that more than three-quarters of Sherman Williams paint stores were located within 5 miles of a Home Depot store.

Location data can be useful for merger analysis. If a merger creates too high of a share in a market that can be a drawback for antitrust approval. On the positive side, a large overlap among factor locations or warehouses could signal sizable potential cost synergies. Combining mapping with demographic data provides additional insights into the economics of expansion. Shopping malls covering geographies with higher population density and income levels are more desirable than malls in rural areas. For retailers, are new stores being added in regions with lower population densities and income levels than the corporate average? Are new stores getting closer together, indicating a greater risk of cannibalization? Is the mix of outlet stores increasing, portending a lower margin mix?

Cell towers receive signals from all devices - most importantly our phones, which have almost become a personal appendage. Teralytic has partnered with telecom operators to analyze aggregated and anonymized data from hundreds of millions of mobile phone users. For travel, data could reveal traffic on toll roads, the impact of high-speed trains on the share of rail passengers between cities, traffic congestion, and even the mix of foreign versus domestic travelers. For retail, mobile data could show a store or mall's catchment area (from how far away does the store draw customers), how much time customers spend in a store or mall, and even whether the customer is using the internet in the store. For restaurants, the mobile data could indicate when diners frequent the location, peak versus off-peak demand, and whether new products or promotions were affecting the share of breakfast or lunch traffic.

Improving hardware has enabled satellites to provide pictures in greater detail, and smarter software enables computers to interpret the pictures with greater accuracy. By taking pictures of Chinese manufacturing facilities, SpaceKnow can more quickly and objectively gauge China's manufacturing production trends than official data. Using drones, balloons, satellites and geolocation, Orbital Insight is probably most applicable for defense and government planning purposes, but investors could use its services to gauge oil supply through satellite pictures of drilling activity and oil stored in floating tankers, and pictures of parking lots would reveal customer traffic at stores, malls and theme parks. Finally, by combining weather data with location mapping, investors can quickly determine which companies are most impacted by weather disruptions like floods, blizzards, and hurricanes.

Regulatory Data

Obtaining data to predict government actions can be difficult. FiscalNote collects and organizes legislative and regulatory data on the local, state and federal level, plus applies artificial intelligence to predict outcomes. Applications could involve drugs, rate cases, gaming and rate cannabis. By analyzing past votes from regulators, investors could better predict FDA drug approvals or rate cases for electricity (typically public utility commissions), natural gas (Federal Energy Regulatory Commission) or railroad rates ((Surface Transportation Board). A review of the voting record of legislators could provide clues on the likelihood and timing of approvals for online gaming and cannabis.

ESG - Doing Well by Doing Good

Environmental, Social and Governance (ESG) data refers to metrics related to a company's nonfinancial performance and attributes - a scorecard for stakeholders other than shareholders. ESG metrics can be arbitrary since there are few rules on how they are defined and measured. Morgan Stanley, Sustainalytics, Thomson Reuters and ICE Data Services (in collaboration with BofA Global Research) have attempted to rank companies according to ESG criteria, but no one number can capture the relevance of ESG given that each industry has such different dynamics. However, ICE and Sustainalytics provides very detailed and transparent data on various factors, and the analyst can then determine which factors are most relevant to each stock.

Environmental - Cleaner is More Efficient

Companies that produce goods and materials have a greater impact on the planet than service and software businesses. Consequently, the energy, material, and utility sectors score poorly on environmental metrics in ESG, industrial goods look worse than industrial services, and consumer staples underperform retailing using environmental measures. The Tech sector scores well on most environmental factors because of low direct emissions, but software companies rely on energy-intensive cloud-based data centers and indirectly boost emissions via purchased materials (metals and rare earth minerals) and employment (daily commutes, building maintenance). Electric cars directly produce less greenhouse gas than traditional automobiles, but the benefits are partly offset by the energy needed to charge vehicles and the environmental impact from producing lithium batteries. Although ESG is probably not a good process for comparing service versus goods stocks, goods-producing companies that produce less waste and use less energy than their competitors are probably more efficient and, therefore better-run companies. For example, an airline with a younger fleet would have a better ESG score than one with an older, less fuel-efficient fleet. An industrial or utility that pollutes more would have a greater risk from future lawsuits and environmental remediation costs. Most ESG rankings are heavily weighted by a company's disclosure of ESG data and policies, which favor larger companies, but many environmental factors are quantifiable. ICE and Sustainalytics provide comparative company data on carbon and other greenhouse gas emissions, air and water pollution, fossil fuel and renewable energy use, water efficiency, waste output, recycling, and environmental fines.

Social - Happy Customers and Employees are Good for Profits

Former US Secretary of Treasury Paul O'Neill built his reputation by turning around Alcoa, not by initially emphasizing profit margins but focusing first on safety. O'Neill recognized that a perfect safety record would not only motivate employees but would require them to understand every aspect of the production cycle, which would result in simpler, more efficient operations. ESG data includes workplace injury and fatalities so trends in these metrics could provide early insights into improving or worsening operational efficiency for industrials, materials, and transportation companies.

Changes in product and service quality is another non-financial measure that can foreshadow inflection points in profitability. ESG vendors offer data on product quality, product safety, and operating performance, but many companies provide more industry specific data. The Department of Transportation publishes detailed statistics on airline on-time performance, lost bags, bumped passengers and consumer complaints. An airline whose reliability is deteriorating relative to peers will either lose customers or have to spend more to improve service. Railroads measure locomotive and freight car velocity, dwell time, delays, and idled cars. Warning signs would be a shipper whose velocity is slowing, time that cars are spending in the railyard is rising, delays worsening, and the number of cars sitting idle is increasing. The adoption of precision scheduled rail strategies by Hunter Harrison were instrumental in transforming Canadian National into the highest margin railroad in the world, but the strategy's success first became apparent in the reliability measures.

Happy employees offer better service and provide higher quality goods. Measuring employee engagement appears particularly important in technology, retail, restaurants, and finance because retaining and attracting the best people are critical to performance. Public data reflecting labor morale include employee turnover, fines related to labor practices, training, unionization, and benefits. In addition, Glassdoor collects anonymous review data from current and former employees with workers providing an overall rating and views on career opportunities, CEO performance, culture and compensation levels. Although Glassdoor, like all review sites, appears subject to gaming when a dataset becomes popular, ratings levels and rating changes do appear to have some predictive value, particularly in technology. Glassdoor allows investors to track compensation levels for companies, but I have found that participants often overstate their own incomes on Glassdoor even though the data is anonymous. Datafox (owned by Oracle) and Lusha scrape the web and industry conferences for contact data on public and private companies. Data can be used to determine which companies are attracting and losing employees as well as track the growth of private competitors to public companies, which is important in fragmented industries like trucking or business services. Revelio Labs' workforce data offers insight on ethnic, gender, geographic and skills composition of a company's workforce as well as hiring, attrition, tenure and wage trends.

"We can follow your moral compass as long as it doesn't interfere with my finanacial GPS."

When ranking companies on ESG, many services give US companies with unions a higher score, but I think that is misplaced. In Germany, the unions and management act more as partners, but in the US the relationship is frequently adversarial. That is not to say there are no need for unions. The bargaining power of labor has diminished with globalization and heavily tilted towards companies. Consequently, wages have barely kept pace with inflation over the past few decades and corporate profit margins are at record highs. But happy well-paid employees don't necessarily need unions - so unionization is often a sign that labor relations have already deteriorated. In addition, the nature of union bargaining increases antagonism between labor and management. Strike threats maximize a union's bargaining position, which requires the unions to rally the workforce to support a strike, usually by denigrating a company and its management. My wife used to tell me, don't play rough with the kids before bedtime and expect them to fall asleep. Well, if employees have been told for months that management is unfair, once an agreement is reached, bad feelings don't just disappear but linger long after the contract is signed.

Governance - Important Across all Sectors

Of all the ESG indicators, corporate governance has been shown to be the ESG factor most correlated with performance across all sectors. Governance appears most relevant to businesses where asset allocation decisions are critical to success, such as finance and energy, or that deal with federal, state or municipal agencies. The impact of corporate governance is more evident when things go wrong than when the business runs smoothly. Occurrences of bad governance are not usually isolated events. Red flags include financial restatements, changes in accountants/auditors, too few independent board members, fraud or ethical citations/fines, intercompany transactions, and transactions between the company and management/board members. Too much management/board turnover is bad, but too little often leads to complacency. Equal voting rights ensures shareholders and management interests are aligned, but company founders often demand special voting rights, and many businesses thrive when they have visionary company leaders. However, the skills needed to start a company are often different from the skills needed to run a large organization, and founders are typically slow to cede control.

Risk management is a critical skill and one that sank many financial firms in the Great Financial Crisis. Good management requires the ability to recognize, communicate and neutralize risk. Companies with good risk management have clearly communicated codes of conduct and a culture in which employees feel they can challenge their superiors. In my years at Goldman Sachs, I believed that juniors always felt they could challenge their superiors, and Goldman rarely has suffered big write-offs as frequently as they occurred at the European investment banks. In contrast, companies with larger-than-life CEOs, like Lehman's Dick Fuld, inadvertently intimidate employees and risks recognized from below do not percolate to the top, which ended up sinking banks like Lehman and Merrill. Attending investor meetings with many layers of management can be an effective way of gauging a company's risk culture. Warning signs would be if the CEO dominates the meeting and other executives seem hesitant to chime in the discussion. A good investor meeting highlights the breadth of management talent. Reducing risks is also a good strategy for supply chains and technology. ESG data is available regarding the percentage of supply chain that is covered by industry-recognized supplier codes of conduct, and companies with ethical suppliers have less risk for disruption. ESG vendors track data security breaches and fines, which would highlight companies that are vulnerable to technology disruptions.

Another indication of good governance is management and board composition. A good board has complementary skills that match the needs of the company. One would expect to see electrical engineers on the boards of tech companies, doctors/scientists on the boards of healthcare companies, and MBAs at financials. After a period of market share gains in commercial aerospace and defense, Boeing has suffered a series of setbacks over the past 10 years. Grounding of both the 787 and 737 Max has resulted in Boeing paying big fines to the FAA, compensation to airlines, and share loss to Airbus. Boeing has experienced continual delays on the KC-46A tanker and has fallen far behind SpaceX in the race to fly astronauts to the International Space Station. Bank of America aerospace analyst Ron Epstein has pointed out that Boeing's problems coincide with a change in board composition. Boeing currently has three engineers but no aerospace or mechanical engineers on its board; back in the 1990s, most of its ten-member board had a science background. An effective board must also be diverse, particularly for companies serving a broader population. Women represent a majority of clothing spend, yet it is surprising how few women board members are on company boards. A board composition should probably not be too far off its customer base plus academic research shows that decision-making benefits from a diversity of views.

Compensation - Follow the Money

The annual proxy put to shareholder vote contains information on compensation as well as the backgrounds of boards and management. The structure of compensation informs what management is motivated to achieve. Starting in 2021, 15% of Boeing management pay is linked to quality and safety performance measurements. Prior to 2021, Boeing executives were awarded solely by hitting financial targets, which may have contributed to the company focusing on cost-cutting over product performance. In comparison, Ron Epstein notes that 30% of executive compensation at Lockheed Martin and General Dynamics is tied to strategic and operational performance.

Companies whose compensation plans have a high percentage of variable pay and stock grants typically deliver better and more consistent returns. Stock grants are better than options because options encourage riskier behavior. Be wary of companies in which management pay and stock price performance diverge or where there is a widening spread between management pay and employee compensation. Employees notice when companies give credit to management rather than workers for good performance. Compensation that is tied to revenues and total profits encourages a company to be bigger more than better so compensation tied to return on assets is superior to revenue and EPS (earning per share) superior to overall profit levels. Changes in a compensation plan frequently signal changes in strategic direction. A company switching from incentives based on revenues to one based on margins may be signaling a portfolio restructuring.

Quantitative Analysis - Lies, Damn Lies, and Statistics

The phrase *"There are lies, damn lies and statistics"* was popularized by Mark Twain. Numbers don't lie, but they can be manipulated and are sometimes counterintuitive. For instance, a stock that falls 50%, but then rises 50% is still down 25% from where it started. Statistics are a valuable way to verify whether one's theories regarding relationships are correct, but I am suspicious when people use statistics to try to uncover relationships as the phrase "*correlation does not imply causation*" implies, and I will start this section describing some of the pitfalls of statistics.

I look up in the sky and I see the Big Dipper. It isn't really there but I can't help seeing it. I also can't help making out animals in clouds, the man in the moon, or shapes in inkblots. Humans are hard-wired to find patterns and then make stories to explain them. Like people, computers are programmed to find patterns, and because of their ability to analyze data so much faster than humans, computers are guaranteed to find more patterns, but with less intuition to determine which patterns are real. $E=mc^2$ is a surprisingly simple formula. There is an abundance of data describing the physical universe, but could a computer ever come up with Einstein's theory of relativity or Newton's gravitational formula. Statistical analysis generally applies linear formulas to data, implying each input has a fixed impact for a given increase or decrease in the variable. But why should the effect of a variable be linear and why can't they change over time, particularly for social or economic events? When the impact of input is not equal across all values of an independent variable – for example, a drug losing effectiveness after a certain dosage - statisticians call this heteroscedasticity. Why can't two variables together have a stronger impact together than apart as in chemistry (i.e., epoxy glue). Companies like Kensho and Data Robot are attempting to use artificial intelligence to help analysts integrate data with different frequencies and choose the best regression approach, but I still find humans are better than computers at uncovering formulas. Many of the biotech companies are attempting to use artificial intelligence to find new cancer cures using regressions to uncover new cancer targets, and I hope they prove me wrong, but despite the improvements in computing, the success rate of biotech drugs has barely budged over the decades. Computers are only as smart as the people who program them.

Recursion - Stats when Investors Learn from the Past

Statistics also have difficulty taking into account that relationships evolve over time. Back in the 1990s, I remember a period in which the airlines were enjoying one of those rare periods of rising earnings expectations. Going into the final month of the quarter, airline stocks began to rise as it became clear that earnings were going to exceed estimates. Stocks continue to rise into earnings season as each airline in fact, did beat projections. After the last company reported earnings, all the airline stocks sold off as the catalyst for the buying had now passed. In the next quarter, earnings were again coming in ahead of forecasts and airline stocks started to rise in the final month of the quarter. Once again, stocks continued to climb as airlines beat estimates, but anticipating the post-reporting season sell-off, this time, the stocks began to decline in the middle of the earnings season even as airline earnings posted further earnings beats. In the following quarter of rising earnings expectations, once more airline stocks started to outperform in the final month of the quarter, but on this occasion, stocks started to fall the day prior to the start of earnings season even though once again profits continued to exceed forecasts. The lesson is that investors do learn from the past, and any formula that wants to predict behavior has to take into account that investors will adjust their behavior in response to each interaction. Computer scientists call this recursion, which means that the equation an analyst creates to make a prediction must include a copy of itself within the equation, creating a continual loop of predictions. Or, as Mark Twain purportedly opined, *"History doesn't repeat itself but it often rhymes."*

Timing of Cause and Effect Can Vary

Regressions not only assume that the impact of a variable is constant, but that the timing of the impact is also constant. The stock market anticipates turning points in cyclical earnings, but sometimes the lead time is two quarters and sometimes stock prices tend to rebound more than a year in advance of an economic recovery. Regressions often assume a constant lead time and may understate the power of a relationship. For example, a drug may work faster on an empty stomach than after a meal, or the lead time from an upturn in corporate profits can have a faster impact on capital spending when margins are relatively low. Charts often do a better job of revealing relationships than regressions because one can visually see the effect of a variable even if the timing of the impact is not consistent. Perhaps when performing statistical analysis, one should have the lead time itself tied to an independent variable.

Collinearity - Teasing out Relationships

The Southwest Airlines effect as documented by the Department of Transportation in the 1980s, demonstrated that adding flights and dropping fares stimulated traffic. In markets where Southwest cut prices by 50%, demand more than doubled. A similar effect has been shown in Europe from Ryanair. Yet, if you run a regression of volume versus price for airline travel overall, the relationship isn't nearly as strong. Similarly, rising oil prices are clearly negative for airlines, yet the simple correlation between oil prices and airline stocks is negligible. In both cases, the problem with simple regressions is that another factor is influencing both sides of the equation in the same direction. Both oil prices and airline stocks are cyclical so when the economy is strong, oil prices and airline stocks tend to rise. Similarly, when the economy is strong, traffic demand rises, enabling airlines to raise fares. Statisticians call this collinearity - when an outside variable has a direct impact on both factors being tested.

Statisticians recognize the pitfalls of regressions and use a variety of methods to prevent overfitting - creating a formula with too many variables that works for historic data but ends up not being predictive. In Ridge or Lasso regressions, penalties are added for each variable to make equations less complex - simplifying to prevent overfitting (making an equation fit past data too tightly so that its predictive power deteriorates). With Lasso regressions, adjustments are made to ensure that additional variables don't dilute the importance of the primary variables. Principal components analysis (PCA) standardizes data so variables with greater ranges don't dominate and use linear algebra instead of regressions to rank variables by importance and discard less effective ones while partial least squares is similar to PCA but add exponents to the variables.

Despite the power of statistics, often human intuition is just as effective. To adjust for the economy's effect on both oil and airline stocks, rather than use these statistical techniques to uncover formulas, I simply compared how airline stocks performed relative to the Morgan Stanley Cyclical Index when oil prices rose and fell. As one would expect, airline stocks outperformed cyclical stocks when oil fell and underperformed when oil pricesd rose - oil price alone contributed to more than half of the relative movement of airline stocks. To measure price elasticity, I compared how much airline traffic outpaced industrial production versus how much prices outpaced inflation. I used industrial production rather than GDP since business travel accounts for more than half of airline revenues and business travel spend is more volatile than leisure. Once again, the correlation strengthened considerably and showed that a 10% drop in price leads to a similar increase in volume.

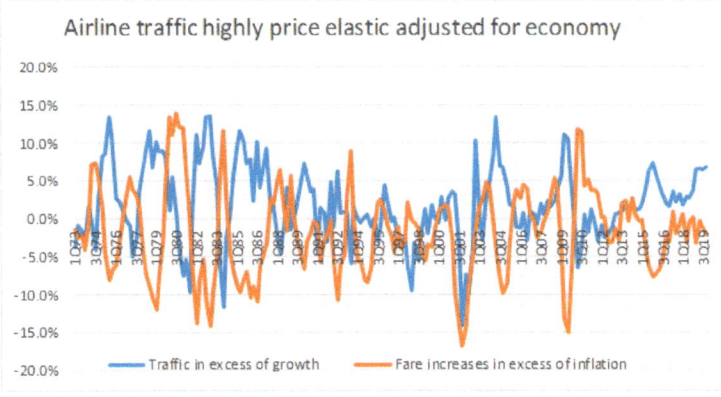

Source: Airlines for America.

Natural Language Processing - Computerized Sentiment

Natural Language Processing (NLP) uses machine learning techniques to convert text into measures of sentiment and create sentiment indicators by counting positive and negative words. What is intuitive to humans is not intuitive to computers and the computer must be trained to understand the word in context. For example, the word cost and risk are negative but not if decreasing is put in front of them. When used on a history of earnings transcripts, NLP can determine if companies are becoming more or less optimistic over time or even more evasive as a signal for turning points. Investing clients are applying NLP on analyst reports in the same fashion because analysts are very deliberate in changing ratings and the tone of the report changes months before analysts raise or cut their ratings.

Quantifying Portfolio Risk

Factor investing, often called Smart Beta, is the use of quantifiable characteristics to categorize stocks and choose those with the most desirable qualities. Unfortunately, predicting which factors will outperform is no easier than predicting earnings or stocks. However, analyzing a portfolio through a factor lens is useful for all portfolio managers. When constructing a portfolio, an analyst evaluates each stock on its own merits, but collectively the portfolio may reveal unconscious biases, and factor analysis can uncover whether a portfolio is too tied to a particular characteristic. Factors can be categorized as value, growth, beta, momentum, GARP (growth at a reasonable price), leverage, quality, short interest, stock price, margin, dividend yield, duration, and most recently, ESG.

Value and growth are some of the most popular factors but can be defined in many ways. Portfolio managers measure value using multiples of earnings (P/E), EBITDA (earnings before interest, taxes, depreciation and interest), book value, and sales. Growth is characterized by longer-term sales or earnings trends. As defined by low P/E, value stocks have outperformed over time, but have underperformed in the past decade. Of course, earnings aren't always predictable, and a stock that looks cheap because estimates are overly optimistic is called a *"value trap."* Value stocks tend to be more cyclical so they often perform poorly during recessions and outperform during recoveries. Growth stocks work best in environments of modest growth and low inflation.

Beta is a measure of stock volatility, and growth investors often penalize faster-growing stocks if they have a higher risk. Stocks with high beta often perform worst at the start of a bear market and perform best early in a bull market. Beta is often equated with risk and usually, stocks with greater risk are more volatile, but beta measures a stock's price volatility relative to the market and not in absolute terms so a company can be quite risky and have a low beta if its price moves are uncorrelated with the overall market. GARP is an attempt to combine growth and value strategies by dividing the earnings or sales multiple by the growth rate. Quality quantitative investors seek stocks with higher margins, better balance sheets and more consistent earnings.

Momentum has consistently been demonstrated to be an effective factor. Momentum can be based on movements in the stock price or earnings estimates. Stock charts are a method of measuring momentum. Leverage has been a useful factor in the past few decades as stocks with low leverage have outperformed the market, but this can be partly explained by the outperformance of technology stocks, which tend to have little debt. Some quants use changes in short interest as a means of momentum, but selling stocks that have rising short interest proved quite risky during the 2021 retail swarm into meme stocks. Equity duration and dividend yield factors are tied to interest rates. Duration measures the sensitivity of a stock to changes in interest rates, and stocks with high dividend yields perform best in periods of low and falling rates.

Valuation – Good Companies are not Always Good Stocks

The longer your investing timeframe, the less valuation matters, but in the short-to-intermediate term, good companies are not always good stocks if they get too expensive and bad companies can be good stocks if they get too cheap. If company financials were easy to predict accurately, then valuation would be the primary driver of stock prices, but the degree of estimate accuracy is not very high and becomes exponentially less reliable as you move further into the future. If a stock looks cheap, the market may be temporarily inefficient but is more likely to indicate that earnings expectations are overly optimistic. Valuation is less of an endpoint and more of a starting point to help one pinpoint where one's estimates or consensus estimates could be mistaken.

In a world of perfect information, the purest way of valuing stocks is by focusing on free cash flow - either by performing discounted cash flow (DCF) analyses or comparing on multiples of free cash flow, such as stock price divided by free cash flow per share or total capitalization (EV or enterprise value, which combines the market value of debt and equity) divided by free cash flow before financing costs. The next best methodology is to compare on the basis of earnings (P/E or EBITDA) followed by revenue and book value. Unfortunately, as one moves up the chain of valuation techniques, the degree of estimate accuracy becomes less reliable.

Cash Flow Analysis is Best for Biotech, Energy/Minerals, and Real Estate

To obtain a DCF value, an analyst must calculate the following components: free cash flow (comprised of earnings, changes in working capital, non-cash expenses, cash taxes and capital expenditures) over a forecast period, steady-state free cash flow, discount rate (sum of the risk-free rate, equity market risk premium, company risk relative to the market), and terminal growth rate. Terminal means forever, which is a long time and well beyond any analyst's mental capacity. Usually, the terminal value (value of the free cash flows beyond the forecasted period) is more than two-thirds of the total DCF value, so a longer forecast period prior to calculating a terminal value is better. Eventually, all businesses mature, so applying a terminal growth rate above nominal GDP growth (3%-4%) or a terminal value multiple above the S&P 500 is aggressive.

Working capital is simply the difference between how fast a company collects its bills versus how quickly it pays its bills, and changes to working capital should be relatively low when a company reaches maturity. Most companies make their goods or perform their services prior to getting paid, and working capital tends to be a negative cash flow item during a period of growth and a source of cash during a period of shrinkage. However, for software companies that collect annual subscription fees up front, working capital is a source of funds. In the long run, capital spending should slightly exceed depreciation owing to inflation, but for companies that have completed acquisitions, the non-cash amortization can meaningfully boost cash flow. I object to the practice of adding back non-cash stock compensation to calculate free cash flow. A company that pays its CEO $1 million in stock is in the same position as a company whose CEO receives $1 million in cash and then purchases $1 million of new stock from the company, yet the DCF would assign a much higher value to the first company if you add back stock compensation unless you take into account all the new shares that will be issued over time.

The calculation of the rate used to discount cash flows is more straightforward. The 30-year US bond is a good proxy for a long-term risk-free rate, and the equity risk premium implied by the level of the stock market indices generally ranges from 5%-6%. To account for the additional risk adjustment for an individual stock, analysts typically multiply the market risk premium by beta, which is the degree to which the stock moves when the market rises and falls. I don't believe beta captures the true volatility of a company. Beta is measured over a relatively short time span and doesn't necessarily capture the risk over the course of a cycle. In addition, beta captures sensitivity to market moves but not company-specific risks. Stocks with binary outcomes may be relatively stable for long periods of time until the event occurs and their correlation with market moves is low, yet these are risky companies. Using a measure of earnings volatility rather than correlation to market moves seems a better way to arrive at a discount rate.

Healthcare analysts value small and midcap biotech stocks using DCFs because the companies develop a finite number of drugs that can be modeled out to the expiration of the patent. Health agencies provide good data on the number of people suffering from the ailment the drug will treat, and market penetration is a function of the effectiveness of the drug, the number of competing treatments, the number of doses, treatment length, and prices of comparable treatments. The cost of goods sold depends on the royalties needed to be paid if the drug was acquired or jointly discovered and the complexity of the manufacturing process- biological drugs are more difficult to make than small molecule drugs.

Many analysts only deduct the R&D required to gain approval of the drug being modeled and exclude the R&D from other efforts that could result in additional revenue streams. Upon patent expiration, competition from generics is anticipated to dramatically impact the drug's price and sales volume; consequently, little terminal value is awarded for off-patent small molecule drugs that can easily be copied by generic manufacturers. Because biological drugs are more difficult to copy, analysts assume a somewhat more gradual decline in cash flow, and gene therapy is assumed to have the longest cash flow tail.

Of course, the biggest challenge for biotech investors is determining whether a drug will actually work. Drug testing goes through five phases. Drugs are first tested in the petri dish or on nonhumans (preclinical), then tested on healthy people to determine dosing and safety (Phase 1), then tested for side effects and efficacy (phase 2 and then a larger/longer phase 3 study), and finally upon approval post-marketing monitoring for long-term side effects and efficacy. Studies indicate that only 10%-15% of drugs entering phase 1 eventually receive approval with a much higher success rate for vaccines treating infectious diseases and a much lower rate for cancer treatment, which is why biotech investors prefer to own a basket of biotech stocks. Once in phase 2, the odds of approval rise to 25%-30%, and phase 3 probabilities climb to 60%-65%.

Analysts start by applying these probabilities to their DCFs, but I have perceived a Lake Wobegon effect (where all children are above average), so slightly higher probabilities are typically applied. In my experience, drugs for diseases that are well understood or where drugs with similar mechanisms of action have demonstrated success deserve above-average probabilities, but drugs for less well-understood diseases (Alzheimer and many cancers) or for diseases that are difficult to diagnose (NASH, a liver disorder) warrant below average probabilities. Often a drug will not meet its threshold for the initial targeted population but will show greater efficacy in subsets of the population. Given that normal randomness would result in variation among subsets, this cherry-picking of data deserves to be assigned lower probabilities of success.

DCF valuation is also conducive to energy and mining stocks because the wells or mines have defined production lives and pipeline companies have set contracts. Although predicting oil, natural gas, and metals prices is fraught with risk, energy and mining stocks should be operating on the same set of expectations as future market prices for oil, gas, and metals. Plugging in futures' price assumptions indicates whether the equity markets are attractively priced relative to the hard commodities. Current production rates and unit production costs provide a good starting point for predicting volumes and expenses, but the productivity of mines and oil wells decline over time, particularly with the advent of fracking. On the other hand, if one only gives credit for existing reserves, the capital spending to develop reserves should also decline over time. Geography also plays a role in energy and mining stocks. Reserves in countries with the strong rule of law are considered less risky and deserve a lower discount rate than reserves in developing nations with higher political uncertainty.

The value of oil stocks relative to oil prices has declined over the past decade, implying that the market currently assigns a lower terminal value to oil stocks, which is consistent with the view that the need to address climate change will result in a sharp drop off in oil demand over the next 15-20 years. This drop off in demand is not likely to be linear but gain steam towards the end of the decade. However, climate change regulations are likely to impede production as well as demand so prices could remain sticky in the interim.

Of all sectors, real estate probably has the most predictable cash flows, but rather than use DCFs, and most REIT analysts use cap rates. There are a large number of real estate transactions, which provide a current view of valuation. Cap rates are defined as the operating income of a property divided by its market value - in effect, an inverse of a free cash flow multiple (Market value divided by FCF) - so a lower cap rate means a higher valuation. Cap rates are sensitive to changes in macro factors such as interest rates, but also location and use. Higher density locations tend to have lower cap rates. Data centers and industrial use currently have lower cap rates than retail and senior living.

P/E and EV/EBITDA - Preferred Measure for Mature Companies

When valuing more established companies, most analysts use either multiple of earnings per share (P/E) or multiples of EBITDA (essentially cash flow prior to financing costs). Generally, analysts use P/E (stock price dividend by earnings) for companies whose earnings are more predictable and EV/EBITDA (enterprise value divided by earnings before interest, taxes, depreciation and amortization) for companies that are more cyclical. EV/EBITDA is also the preferred measure for companies with more leverage, which increases the variability of returns.

Consequently, the more consistent railroads stocks are valued using P/E as compared to the volatile airline stocks that are valued using EBITDA. Analysts rely on P/E for tech hardware, but EV/EBITDA for industrials; P/E for business services and payments, but EBITDA for media; P/E for Walmart and Target versus EV/EBITDA for department stores; P/E for medical devices and diagnostic equipment companies versus EBITDA for hospitals; P/E for consumer staples and discretionary companies such as Nike, but EBITDA for hotels and restaurants; P/E for utilities, but EBITDA for homebuilders and building products; and P/E for auto dealers, but EBITDA for manufacturers of autos and auto parts.

EBITDA better measure than P/E		
Debt	0	800
Depreciation	50	50
Pretax, pre-interest	125	125
Interest	0	40
Pretax income	125	85
Income taxes	25	17
Net earnings	100	68
P/E	16	16
Market cap	1600	1088
Enterprise value	1600	1888
EV/EBITDA	9	11
P/E assuming same EV/EBITDA		12

Imagine two companies with identical returns excluding interest expense, but the first company has no debt and the second one has $800mn of debt. The company with no debt accrues $50mn of depreciation, makes $100mn of net profits, and trades at $1.6bn, implying a P/E of 16x and EV/EBITDA of 9x. The second company incurs $40mn of interest (assuming 5% cost of debt), resulting in the company having $68mn of net earnings (assuming 20% tax rate.) If that company traded at 16x earnings, then the market capitalization would equal $1.1bn and enterprise value (sum of the market value of equity and debt minus cash) total $1.9bn. This suggests that the same cash flows of the second company are worth more than the first, which seems illogical and why private equity firms focus on EV/EBITDA. More likely, the second company's enterprise value would also total $1.6bn, which would imply an equity value of $800mn, or 12x earnings and explains why companies with more leverage tend to have lower P/E multiples.

To assign the proper multiple to apply to earnings, one must start by determining the proper market multiple. A good rule of thumb for calculating the market multiple is the Rule of 21, in which the market's P/E multiple over time has equaled 21 minus the rate of inflation. Consistent with this rule, inflation has climbed around 2% per annum over the past decade, and the market multiple has averaged 19x earnings and 11x-12x EBITDA. In a DCF, the multiple of FCF is calculated by dividing by the cost of capital minus the free cash flow growth rate. The Rule of 21 implies that as inflation rises, the free cash flow growth rate will lag the increase in the cost of capital, which intuitively makes sense since the replacement cost of equipment and inventory will be higher than the accounting cost.

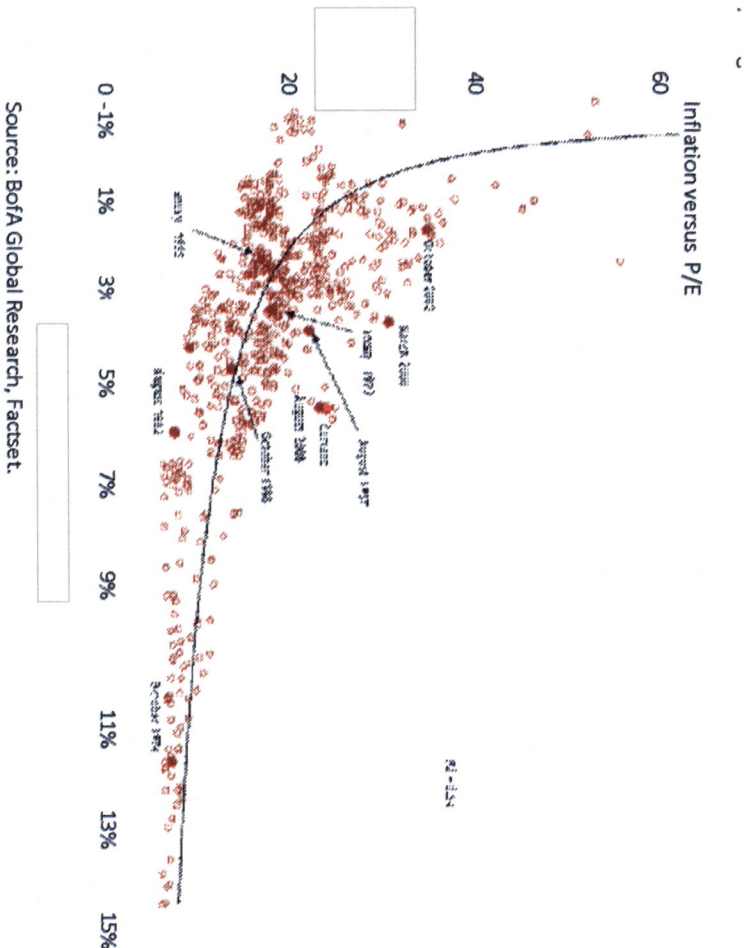

Source: BofA Global Research, Factset.

Companies with earnings growth higher than the market trade at a premium to the market, and those with slower earnings growth trade at a discount. The premium is proportional to a company's three to five-year growth rate and is called a PEG (P/E Growth) ratio. Over the past few decades, the PEG ratio has been approximately 1.5x-2.0x, so a company growing 20% warrants a 35x P/E multiple. Companies also trade at a higher P/E or EBITDA multiple if their businesses have a higher FCF conversion (free cash flow as a percentage of earnings) or less volatile earnings streams. Consequently, businesses that are less capital intensive, less cyclical, and relatively debt-free tend to trade at a premium to the market.

Some larger established companies, most frequently in the industrial and utility sectors, are composed of different subsidiaries, which have different growth and risk characteristics. For these companies, analysts employ a sum of the parts (SOTP) valuation for each of the distinct businesses. Unless there are obvious synergies from the pieces, the market rarely gives full value to the parts (analysts term this a conglomerate discount) until management explicitly states that pieces will be sold or spun off.

Definition of Earnings has Become Opaque

An increasing challenge for arriving at a P/E multiple is that there is no longer a uniform definition of earnings or even EBITDA. GAAP (Generally Accepted Accounting Principles) required by the SEC in audited financial statements are consistent across companies, but valuation should reflect the underlying cash earnings of a company and therefore exclude non-recurring items that distort a company's true earnings power. For this reason, companies often provide their own view of *"operating earnings"* or *"cash earnings"* in their releases, which can exclude a host of items - stock compensation, merger-related amortization of intangibles, damage from hurricanes and other weather events, gains/losses from the sale of subsidiaries or assets, factory or store openings and closings, bad debt expense, inventory write-downs, accounting adjustments from previous under or over accruals, regulatory fines, back-dated labor settlements, and legal suits. When investors want to view consensus earnings expectations, they usually employ the services of an aggregator (i.e., Bloomberg, First Call, Visible Alpha), which try to gather all the estimates using similar definitions of earnings on their primary screen. Since analysts want to show how their estimates compare to what the company is expected to report, the company in effect determines what is considered *"operating earnings."* Quantitative strategists typically use more conservative accounting and measure the difference between GAAP and analyst estimates, which have been rising over time, indicating a gradual decline in the quality of earnings. When comparing multiples of earnings or EBITDA, differences in quality of earnings need to be taken into account by awarding a lower multiple to lower quality earnings or making adjustments to earnings so that all companies are on the same *"operating earnings"* standard. A sign of lower quality earnings is when a company seems to take out one-time items nearly every quarter. One method of adjusting *"operating earnings"* is to average out the annual non-recurring

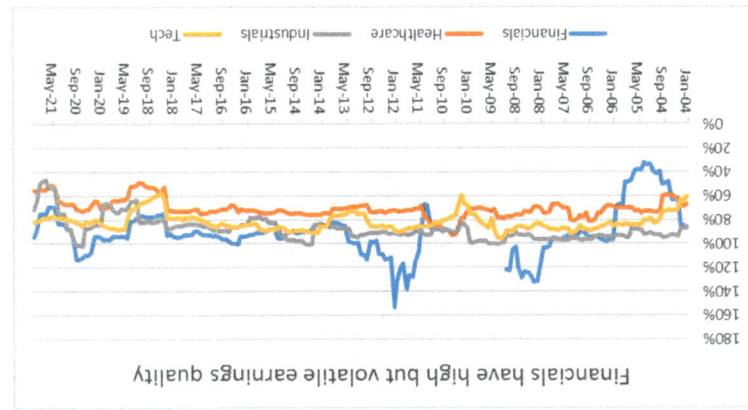

Financials have high but volatile earnings quality

Over the past decade, earnings quality has trended downward, a sign of frothiness in the market. During the brief COVID-induced recession, earnings quality dropped sharply but has rebounded with economic recovery. Among sectors, financial stocks have generally posted the highest quality of earnings over the past few decades, but typically suffer the steepest decline during recessions, yet the sector's earnings quality held up well in 2020. The tech sector has demonstrated the most consistent earnings quality over the past few decades and the level of tech earnings quality has improved relative to other sectors — another justification for rising tech multiples. In contrast, the quality of earnings in healthcare has consistently fallen below other sectors.

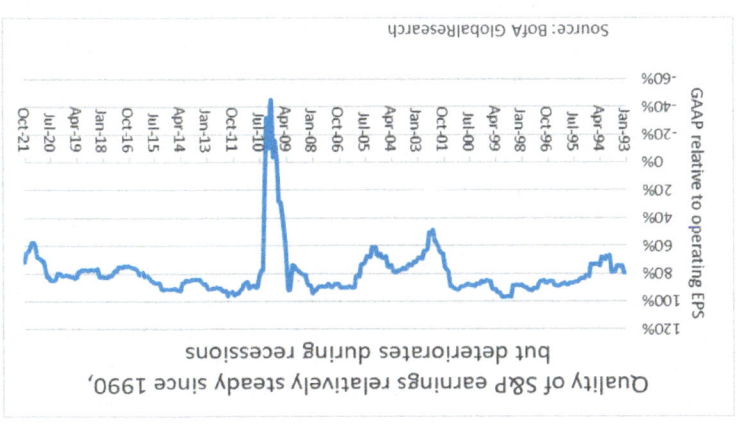

Quality of S&P earnings relatively steady since 1990, but deteriorates during recessions

Source: BofA GlobalResearch

items over the past five years and deduct that from earnings to arrive at true earnings power.

Valuation of Cyclical Stocks

Imagine a company that consistently delivers $5 per share a year and another that alternately delivers $9 per share and then $1 per share. In the long run, both companies will produce the same earnings and should have similar stock prices though in reality, the market will probably award a slightly lower multiple to the second, less consistent company. If the first company's stock trades at $90, the second company's stock should trade at 10x earnings in the good years and 90x earnings in the bad years. This is the challenge for cyclical stocks - multiples compress near earnings peaks and expand during earnings troughs. Investors don't want to pay too high a multiple when times are good, but don't want to undervalue the stock when a company's fortunes temporarily turn sour. However, unlike our artificial example, analysts don't know what peak level of earnings can be achieved during an economic recovery nor how low they can sink during a recession.

Analysts tend to have different approaches depending on the stage of the cyclical recovery. When earnings are falling and multiples expand during a recession, analysts' average multiples that were achieved at the troughs of past cycles and apply them to their estimate of the current cycle's bottom. If this calculation implies little further downside risk, then stock ratings are upgraded. Early in the recovery, analysts shift to a normalized earnings approach. To arrive at an estimate of normalized earnings, analysts either take the average earnings over the entire previous cycle or simply take the midpoint between the last cycle's peak and trough. In this case, multiples achieved during the mid-cycle of past recoveries are applied. In the latter stages of a cyclical recovery, analysts apply the relatively low average late-cycle multiples to their estimates of peak profits to determine how much further upside is possible.

Inevitably during a recovery, management or analysts make a claim that this time is different and their business has become less cyclical and therefore deserving of a higher multiple. After a period of consolidation and higher earnings, US airlines made this claim in both the 1990s and 2010s, but markets remained skeptical and airlines continued to trade at 50% below market multiples with the pessimism proving to be justified owing to 9/11 and COVID-19. Railroad consolidation and improved efficiencies resulted in higher profits during the 1990s, but multiples did not respond until after the rails delivered consistent profits throughout the 2001 recession. Railroad stocks began to close the valuation gap with the market in the 2000s and now trade in line with the market having also performed relatively well during the Great Financial Crisis. British Air and Singapore traded at a premium to global airline stocks in the 1990s after remaining profitable during the 1990 recession, but that premium disappeared in the 2000s when their margins dropped back down to the industry average. Given the relative outperformance of tech earnings during the brief 2020 downturn, tech valuations are likely to remain elevated until proven otherwise in the next recession.

Sales Multiples for High Growth Companies

For immature, fast-growing companies, near-term earnings and cash flow do not capture their potential earnings power, and technology is changing so quickly that forecasts of out-year profits are too speculative to provide a firm foundation for valuation. Analysts rely on multiples of sales for these types of companies, particularly in the software, internet, diagnostics, and medical device sectors, but also some consumer innovators like Beyond Meat and Oatly.

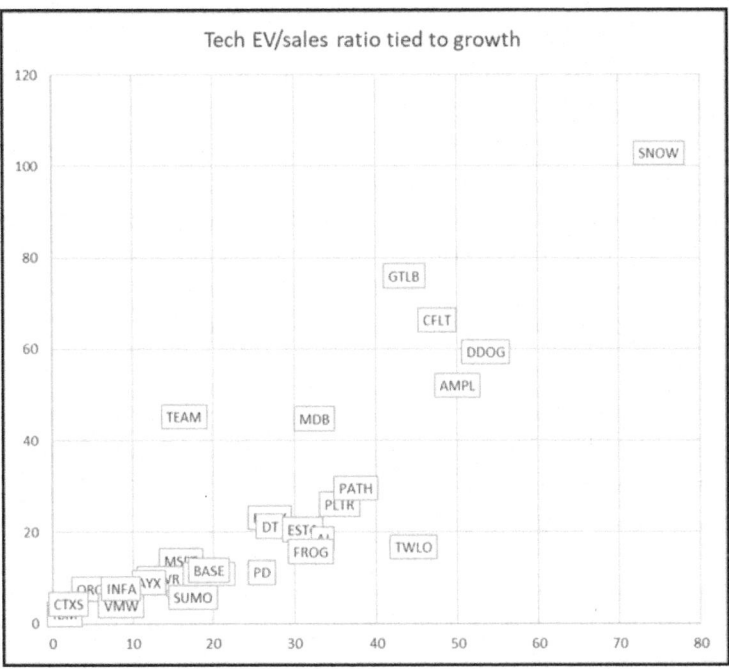

Similar to the PEG ratio for mature companies, EV/sales multiples for these fast-growing sectors are proportional to their growth rates. These companies rarely have much debt, but enterprise value is used to adjust for differences in cash holdings. In the past couple of years, software and diagnostics companies have traded at sales multiples that are 0.6x-1.0x their three-year growth rate, while internet and medical device companies have generally traded at multiples that are 0.3x-0.5x sales growth. While growth is the dominant determinant of sales multiples, valuation for these companies is affected by the market size (TAM or total available market). Innovative companies targeting huge potential markets (such as Guardant Health for cancer tests or Schrodinger for drug discovery) are rewarded with much higher multiples than companies with more narrowly defined markets, which is often the case for medical devices. For software companies like Bill.com and Coupa, large potential markets indicate that above-average growth can be sustained for longer periods of time and therefore deserve higher multiples.

Operating and gross margins can also influence sales multiples. Software companies are more easily scaled than companies producing or retailing products and have higher gross margins, which enables them to have greater earnings leverage as revenues scale. Software companies also have lower capital spending needs so can generate stronger cash flows as they scale. Analysts differentiate companies by comparing the cost of acquiring customers with the value generated during a typical customer's lifetime. Internet companies tend to have to spend more to drive customer value over time than software. Bank of America insurance analyst Josh Shanker's analysis of Lemonade and Root indicated that insurtech companies also have uninspiring customer economics. Like many fintech companies, they have relatively high customer acquisition costs, and the churn rate is high because customers are price-sensitive rather than brand loyal.

One challenge particularly related to internet and software valuations is the practice of deliberately providing overly conservative guidance so that management can show they consistently beat expectations. Analysts are reluctant to produce forecasts much higher than guidance, particularly for companies that have recently gone public because there is little financial history and company managements get upset if analysts set too challenging targets. In these cases, valuations appear overly expensive because investor expectations (called whisper estimates) are much higher than consensus forecasts. Many less mature, fast-growing companies eventually are acquired by larger companies, which have stronger distribution and are better able to leverage the technology. These companies can also trade at higher multiples than their financials would seem to warrant. The diagnostics, medical device and software sectors are especially acquisitive.

Book Value Benchmark for Financials

Similar to other cyclical stocks, earnings in the financial sector can be quite choppy and earnings multiples compress during good times and expand during bad times. Commercial and consumer banks took huge write-offs during the pandemic year 2020, only to reverse those accruals in 2021 so neither year reflects the true steady-state earnings power of the company. Insurers experience earnings volatility as catastrophic losses vary significantly from year to year. Analysts can exclude write-offs to get some sense of underlying profits, but making smart loans and insurance bets is what separates good and bad banks and insurers. As with other cyclicals, analysts must make some adjustments to normalize earnings and applying the average loss ratio over the course of the cycle offers a good approximation.

Rather than P/E, investors focus on Price/Book Value (P/BV) for most financial stocks, particularly during periods of elevated write-offs, partly because book value is a less volatile metric, but also because financial regulations limit a company's potential earnings power by tying its available assets under risk to its equity cushion. The multiples of book value the market assigns financial stocks is directly related to their return on equity or capital (ROE or ROIC), especially bank stocks (Chart). Stocks that don't earn their cost of capital (currently 8%-10%) trade at a discount to book value and correlations indicate that the P/BV multiple rises 0.1x for each percentage point the bank trades above its book value. As with P/E, calculating a P/BV using a normalized level of returns gives one a truer sense of a stock's worth.

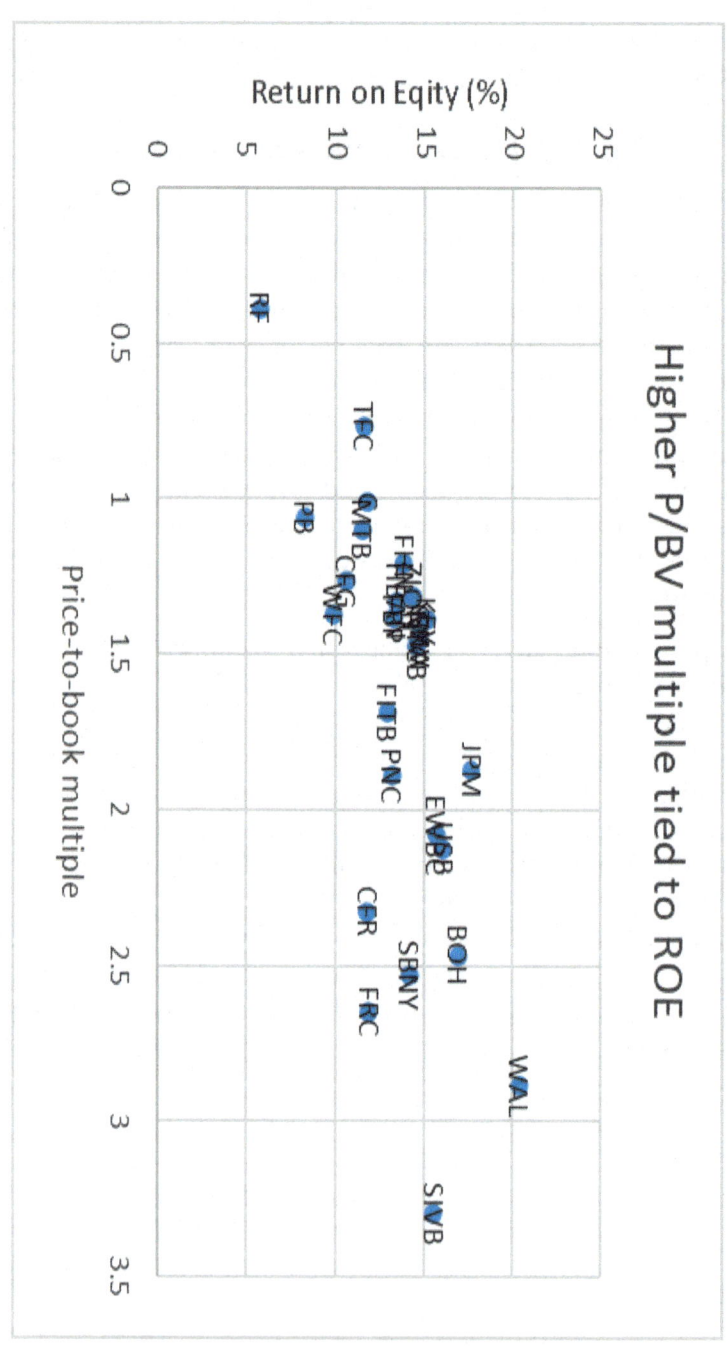

Option Value - Something from Nothing

In the 1990s, I noticed a curious phenomenon among airline stocks. When industry leader American announced an equity raise, AMR stock fell because of the dilution to shareholders, but when financially strapped TWA announced an equity raise, the stock climbed. In addition, I noticed that when airlines and steel stocks suffered large losses or were even in bankruptcy, the stocks still had some value. Finally, in contrast to other sectors, highly leveraged airlines like USAir traded at a premium to airlines with better balance sheets, such as Delta. How to make sense of this?

My explanation is that all stocks have an option value, which typically is small relative to their intrinsic value. An option that is out of the money - the right to buy a stock at a level (called the strike price) that is currently above the market - always has value because there is a chance that fortunes will change more than expected and lift the stock above the strike price before the option expires. In option pricing models, an option expiring in 12 months is worth more than an option expiring in 3 months and an option on a volatile stock is worth more than an option on a stable one. Returning to my airline example, AMR stock fell when it issued equity because its intrinsic value per share fell as more stock was issued. On the other hand, investors feared that TWA could go bankrupt and was on borrowed time. TWA had little intrinsic value at that time and its option value increased when it issued stock because the cash inflow extended its expiration date. Since greater leverage leads to greater volatility, US Airways had more option value than Delta; or put another way, an investor who was bullish on airlines would receive more bang for the buck buying a lower quality airline than a high-quality one.

There is always some chance that stocks undergoing Chapter 11 will have value after emerging from bankruptcy (Hawaiian Airlines last decade and Hertz are the most recent examples) so even the stocks of bankrupt companies trade at positive values. To calculate option value, I create a probability tree starting with a baseline estimate and tabulating possible outcomes utilizing historical variation in estimates. If a one standard deviation move (equivalent to one-third probability) in EBITDA equals $100 million and a two-standard move (5% probability) equals $200 million, I take the baseline estimate going out three years and record the possible outcomes (baseline plus three $200 million upside moves being the least likely), assign a value (multiplying EBITDA by late-cycle airline multiples) for each outcome, and weight that value by its probability (less than 1% for the most bullish outcome.) Since an option cannot be worth less than $0, I place a zero value for all negative outcomes and add up the probability-weighted positive outcomes to arrive at a rough estimate for a stock's option value - no matter how improbable, a stock is always worth something.

Option tree - something from nothing

Year 1 Outcomes	Year 2 Outcomes	Year 3 Outcomes	Probability Weighted Outcome	Value Contribution
		200	3.703704	14.81481481
		100	0.462963	1.851851852
		200	3.703704	14.81481481
100	100	100	7.407407	29.62962963
		0	0	0
		100	1.851852	7.407407407
	0	0	0	0
		-100	0	0
		200	3.703704	14.81481481
	100	100	7.407407	29.62962963
		0	0	0
		100	7.407407	29.62962963
0	0	0	0	0
		-100	0	0
		0	0	0
	-100	-100	0	0
		-200	0	0
		100	0.462963	1.851851852
	0	0	0	0
		-100	0	0
		0	0	0
-100	-100	-100	0	0
		-200	0	0
		-100	0	0
	-200	-200	0	0
		-300	0	0

Option value   150

Avoiding Psychological Mistakes

In the 1990s, Goldman Sachs allowed the research department to make long-short investments using the firm's capital for several years. Research analysts were not compelled to participate and indeed many did not participate. Even analysts who did take part may have waited months between holding positions. Because analysts tend to be too bullish on their sectors, they were forced to go long and short stocks of equal amounts (typically $1 million) within their coverage universe. To be consistent with their ratings, long stocks had to be buy-rated and short stocks neutral or sell-rated. To prevent front-running, an analyst could not raise their rating while holding a long position, nor cut their rating after taking a short position, and they would have to wait a few days after any ratings changes to unwind positions. The research "*hedge fund*" made money every year - $1mn in the first year and $11mn in year 5 - but was finally terminated to avoid any perceptions of conflicts of interest or access to non-public information. Goldman Sachs is a major player in merger and acquisitions, and if any of the long positions were involved in a transaction, the public perception would be negative even though company informational firewalls do keep research unaware of any discussions between the bankers and companies. Goldman's traders were allowed to use firm capital to facilitate transactions with our clients and grew envious that they could not invest the firm's capital unconnected to trades. To appease the traders, equity management relented, but set $100,000 per trader loss limits. However, within a few months, two-thirds of the traders had dropped out and by year end, nearly all had hit their loss limits. I related this anecdote not to claim that Goldman's research analysts were wiser than the traders (Goldman's traders were some of the best in the business), but to highlight some of the psychological pitfalls facing investors.

The Challenge of Being Patient

After the traders had nearly all dropped out, Goldman's head trader told his troops, "There's a lesson here, and it's not that GS research is smarter than GS trading, but that when you go to the track, you don't bet on every race." In other words, research analysts only took positions when they had strong convictions, but traders who make their living being active were taking positions every day. The best blackjack players don't just know when to take a card or hold but also know when to double down or increase their bets when after seeing many cards, they know the remaining deck is in their favor.

Great investors know how to wait. Despite pressures from holding large cash positions in a near zero-rate environment, Berkshire Hathaway can sit on the sidelines for years until a compelling investment opportunity arises and quickly pounce as a result of their financial flexibility, often during recessions or financial crises when other investors are capital constrained. As Berkshire's Warren Buffet says, "The stock market is a device for transforming money from the patient to the impatient." Or, as his partner, Charlie Munger, states more bluntly, "The world is full of foolish gamblers, and they will not do as well as patient investors."

Patience is harder in practice than theory. Try explaining to your boss that you saved him money by doing nothing. Corporate management often complains that Wall Street is too near-term focused, but executives frequently complain about short-term drops in their stock prices (they never seem to complain about short-term pops) that shouldn't matter to them. I remember a United Airlines CFO, Jack Pope telling my mentor, Mike Armellino, that Wall Street is too short-term. Mike queried, "How does United monitor its pension fund performance.?" When the CFO said United reviewed results quarterly, Mike replied, "Well, you're part of the problem." Not only must fund managers exercise patience but so must their investors. Academic research shows that this year's hottest funds are often next year's coldest, and vice versa, but funds with the best near-term track records usually enjoy the highest inflows and funds that have recently performed poorly suffer outflows. So even if a fund manager's strategy is ultimately correct, investor withdrawals may prevent him/her from succeeding. Nassim Taleb's Black Swan strategy (betting on outsized moves in asset prices that inevitably but irregularly occur) has been successful mainly because few investors can wait that long for a payout.

Long-side Traps

When buying stocks, I offer the following advice to avoid falling into the most common behavioral traps:

1) There is a difference between job risk and performance risk.
2) Conventional wisdom is often right, and contrarians are usually wrong.
3) The safest stocks have their own risks.
4) Never wait to buy on dips.
5) Don't wait until you are sure.
6) The longer-term happens sooner than you think.
7) Avoid moving parts.
8) Macro can overwhelm micro.

When analysts make an investment decision, they are taking two types of risk - performance risk and job risk. Performance risk is making poor investment decisions that lead to subpar returns. Job risk is making a decision that costs analysts their jobs. Buying a safe stock, like Apple or Microsoft, comes with some risk of underperformance, but few people will second guess your decision if the stock falters. On the other hand, if an analyst buys a controversial stock, such as an airline or meme equities like GameStop, and the stock falls, his/her judgment will be questioned and the risk of losing one's job is higher. Job risk can cause analysts at buy and sell-side firms to avoid taking on riskier stocks that have attractive returns and put too much faith in widely-owned equities.

Academic research consistently supports the wisdom of crowds, in which the average opinion of a group of not necessarily trained individuals is usually more accurate than an individual expert. On Wall Street, the average forecast of a group of economists is usually more accurate over time than any one individual economist. In a way, the market represents the collective group or conventional wisdom of investors. Consequently, taking a contrarian stance implies that you will usually be wrong, but the returns from taking a correct contrarian stance are often quite lucrative. In contrast, investors will have a higher success rate by purchasing safer stocks, but the returns from being right are relatively low, and the penalty from being wrong are quite high. To sum up, it's OK to be a contrarian but pick your spots carefully. When looking for safe stocks, perhaps the highest returns aren't with the safest, but with relatively safe. When screening for quality, the second quintile ranked stocks may offer higher risk-adjusted returns than the top quintile.

More Certainty, Less Opportunity

The stock market is very efficient. Efficient doesn't mean right, but implies the market is effectively incorporating all known inputs. If an investor waits until he is certain of an outcome, there is probably enough information for many others to come to the same conclusion and the stock will have already priced in the expected outcome. Don't try for A's. Analysts must act when they are 60% sure, not when they are 90% sure. I have generally found that committees are rarely good at building portfolios because by the time you have enough information to convince a committee, the upside for the stock has largely disappeared, and the downside is considerable if there are any negative surprises.

Often if one's confidence in a stock is building, the stock is moving up as well. I often hear buy and sell-side analysts recommend buying the stock on a dip. This rarely works because other investors are also recognizing the improving fundamentals and the stock won't sell off much before someone braver steps in. So don't be cute. If you have enough conviction to buy a stock, the couple of dollars of difference you could save is probably not worth the risk of losing the bigger upside. If you've lost conviction, sell the stock rather than kick yourself for not selling sooner.

Three types of investments I prefer to avoid are cheap stocks that have long-term overhangs, moving parts, and catalysts. The long-term happens sooner than you think, and the markets award lower multiples to stocks with fundamental overhangs long before any impact on earnings. As mentioned before, we will eventually wean ourselves from fossil fuels, and the market will continue to discount energy stocks heavily even though a carbon-free world may be decades away. We are moving to a paperless world and no matter how much paper companies cut capacity, the market won't believe the industry's prosperity can be sustainable. In a world of streaming, the traditional cable will feel continued pressure as well as movie theater chains. The shift to the cloud will continue to weigh on the multiples of companies providing hardware (i.e., Cisco and Oracle) or on-premise service (IBM and SAP). Valuation of mall REITs dipped long before e-tailing had a significant impact on REIT profits, and the threat of Amazon hangs over nearly all companies involved in distribution.

I term *moving parts* investments as companies with businesses moving in separate directions. Often conglomerates have subsidiaries involved in different businesses that are not moving in synchrony. The analyst is trying to determine whether the improving business can outweigh the declining business. When a company's fortune turns, analysts generally underestimate the magnitude of earnings and expecting the profits of the rising subsidiary to outpace the decline in its sinking subsidiary is a difficult calculation. In tech, many companies have a fast-growing cloud business and declining on-premise business or a fast-growing subscription business and a shrinking license business. Valuations for these businesses typically struggle until the business on the rise starts to dwarf in size the falling business. I am also reluctant to invest in stocks with near-term catalysts unless I have some truly unique insight or proprietary information. I think it is arrogant to think that you are smarter than everyone else in predicting highly visible near-term events, and the risks are higher for stocks involved in binary events. Better to spend your energy to predict what will be the next catalyst than predict the outcome of a highly visible one.

Macro Sometimes Overwhelms Micro

Particularly in periods when the monetary authorities are flooding the world with capital, macro factors can overwhelm micro or stock-specific factors. Correlations among asset classes and stocks have increased significantly relative to history, making macro calls as important as stock picking. Although you may choose each stock on its own merits, the portfolio created could include unconscious biases - over or under weighting certain sectors, value versus growth. Large-cap vs small-cap, quality versus cyclical, domestic versus international, high beta or leverage versus lower risk, and dividend yield versus dividend growth. Having a portfolio overly weighted by a factor is not necessarily bad, but one should at least be aware of the risks one is taking and monitor whether a particular factor weighting is impacting performance and why that might persist.

Buying is Easier than Selling

Logically, the decision to sell should be no different than to buy, but in practice, selling is much harder than buying. After a stock is purchased, one becomes emotionally invested in the decision, which makes it harder to reverse. This is particularly true for Wall Street analysts, who have previously published thoughtful reasons to buy a stock and now must publicly explain what caused them to change their mind. Wall Street also has social and economic reasons to favor buy over sell recommendations, and less than 10% of all analyst recommendations are sell or the more euphemistic underperform – Bank of America is one of the few firms to require analysts to have 20% of their stocks rated underperforms.

As an analyst, I spoke with airline management regularly, and the turnover among my company contacts was far less than the turnover among my investor contacts. It is natural to form friendships with your company contacts, which makes one reluctant to be negative. Analysts also receive more buy-side attention when their sector stock prices are rising so bullishness may be part of wishful thinking, which is why analysts are better at picking stocks within their sector than judging whether their group will outperform the market. Deal activity drives investment bank profits, and corporations are less likely to ask a firm with a sell rating to manage their offerings. Investors allocate more commission dollars to analysts that deliver corporate access, and companies prefer to provide access through analysts who are bullish rather than bearish, so even research shops without banking tend to have few negative ratings. Some companies even prevent analysts with sell ratings from asking questions on their earnings calls or put them at the back of the line. So, if regulators want analysts to be more balanced, the government needs to address corporate behavior as much as bankers. While investors criticize analysts for being too bullish, long-only clients become upset when an analyst puts a sell on a stock they own. Hedge funds are more likely to appreciate sell ratings, but only regarding stocks, they don't own or are already short.

Knowing When to Sell

There are many reasons why Investors hold on to their losers for too long. Selling requires one to take action, while being passive is our default. We become vested in the stories that convince us to buy the stock and are reluctant to renounce them. We have a tendency to emphasize new data that fits our theory, dismiss data that counters our theory, or come up with new reasons to support our decision when existing ones prove wrong. I offer the following tips to avoid the pitfalls that prevent us from selling losers.

Clean Slate

For each stock in the portfolio, every month, investors should ask themselves whether they would buy the stock today if it was not in their portfolio. Lee Ainslie, the founder of Maverick Capital, took a slightly different tack. Whenever a stock fell 10%-20% or more, he would sometimes offer the portfolio manager an alternative - either double down or sell out the position. Both approaches try to transform a passive behavior (hold the stock) into an active one, forcing the investor to reevaluate rather than ignore a decision that hasn't yet worked.

Thesis Creep

When an investor purchases a stock, he should write the reasons behind his decision and the factors that would cause him to change his mind on a piece of paper. The paper should be placed in a drawer. After a few months, the investor should take out a new piece of paper, again write down the reasons to own the stock, and then compare it to the list written several months ago. Thesis creep is when you keep changing the reasons to justify a decision, which reflects an emotional or intellectual stubbornness. If the reasons on the two pieces of paper significantly vary, that is a sign that one's investment process is flawed and rationalizing a money-losing investment. For analysts, I recommend having the tone of their reports assessed by machine learning (see pg. on NLP). If the tone of the reports is becoming more negative and the rating hasn't changed, the analyst should strongly consider downgrading the stock.

Cockroach Theory

"Your first loss is your best loss" was a maxim of my favorite Goldman Sachs trader, Andy Berman. When bad news happens and stocks drop sharply in price, investors will typically hold onto the stock because the negative event is now reflected in the share price or perhaps tell themselves they will sell on the bounce. Andy's view was that the drop in the stock price revealed that his reasoning must be wrong and therefore, he should unload the stock because future opportunities to sell would most likely be at lower, not higher prices. A corollary is the cockroach theory, in which one cockroach may be a fluke, but two means an infestation. In my role leading the ratings review committee, I kept track of price objectives changes on buy and sell rated stocks. If analysts lowered their earnings and price objectives twice on a buy-rated stock, the stock continued to underperform the market 75% of the time, yet analysts cut their ratings only 20% of the time. Conversely, if analysts raised their earnings and price objectives twice on an underperform-rated stock, the stock continued to outperform 75% of the time, yet analysts raised their ratings only 30% of the time. The market is efficient at adjusting the stock price to reflect better or worse news, but analysts often fail to recognize that the causes of the disappointments are likely to persist. This applies to cultural issues as well as earnings - analysts were slow at recognizing that Wells Fargo consumer practices were part of a pattern or that European banks write-offs were evidence of persistent risk management issues.

Valuation Alone Rarely a Good Reason to Buy or Sell

No matter how low a stock gets, you can still lose 100%, and the success of momentum as a factor over time indicates that selling a stock that appears expensive can backfire. Investors have been burned shorting expensive stocks like Tesla in the last decade and Amazon in the previous decade. Some stocks trade at high valuations because of their potential to be transformational and will remain expensive as long as that dream remains alive. Despite many years of effort, the large global auto manufacturers still are playing catch up to Tesla in electric car design, and Tesla retains some option value based on Musk's genius. In addition, some stocks are actually worth more as their stock rises. Tesla's high stock price gives the company a financial cost advantage in a capital-intensive industry. Finally, analysts tend to underestimate the magnitude of earnings movements in both directions, so an expensive stock may not end up looking as expensive when earnings are finally reported.

Shorting is Different from Selling

Shorting a stock is simply selling a stock that one doesn't own, but shorting ends up being much harder. For one, shorting requires borrowing a stock, which can become increasingly expensive, particularly for crowded shorts. Shorts are subject to margin calls, which can encourage collective attacks by long-only investors as occurred at meme stocks, such as AMC and GameStop. Nevertheless, stocks with rising short positions usually underperform the market, partly because going shorting requires a lot of conviction. When going long a stock, I'd err on the side of being too early, but for shorting stocks, I'd err on the side of being a little late. The proliferation of ETFs may be increasing the opportunities for short investors. ETFs are not indices but portfolios and an ETF may prove to be a less expensive and more liquid means of shorting its component stocks.

Elements of a Good Stock Pitch

An investment research report or presentation is not a novel but a call to action. Unlike a thriller, the conclusion must be upfront, and you must convince the reader of the reason one should read the report. To do that, your report or presentation must answer one of the following two questions: *"What do I know others don't?"* or *"What do others think that they know that I think is wrong?"* The former is much harder than the latter and requires either a unique set of data, access to information or a novel viewpoint, so most reports focus on where consensus is wrong. A report that I wrote arguing that airline spending was more tied to business than leisure demand and business was much more cyclical than leisure spend would be an example of the latter. Academic writing has different goals than writing for an investment audience, but since we've been taught to write in school, I will organize this section by describing what one might need to unlearn from school.

Don't Waste a Title

Your professor had to read your report, but in the real world, investors are bombarded with thousands of emails a day. Less than 5% of all emails sent by analysts are opened by their clients, less than 1% click on the link to open the report, and of those reading the report, most clients don't even get past the front page. Consequently, the subject lines of emails and the title of the report may be the only chance to grab the reader's attention.

The first page should not only reveal the conclusion but draw the reader in by explaining why they should read the report. The abbreviated answer of my opening question (What do I know others don't and what do others think is wrong) should be presented clearly on the front page. Because analysts know that clients rarely proceed beyond the first page, there is a tendency to put as much as possible on the cover. The reason clients don't go beyond the first page is that they want to obtain the message quickly and decide if they should save the report for when they have time later in the day or week. If too cluttered, they are less likely to read the front page or feel there is less reason to read beyond. Headers throughout the report should enable a reader to skim the report and absorb the major points without having to read the whole text. Too often, analysts put generic titles on their charts and graphs. The title of a chart should explain the point the graphic is trying to make so a client knows the purpose of including the chart. Try to make the reader's experience as easy as possible.

Don't Tell Me What You Know

In school, you get credit for all the facts and points you make, and students have an incentive to put down everything they know in an exam or paper. Biographers have the tendency to include all the details of the subject's life just to show how much effort they have put into the work. In reports and powerpoints, presenters want to show how much they know. Don't tell the audience what you know; just tell them what is important. If the factoid doesn't support the main argument, leave it out. In a presentation Q&A or follow-on call, the client will have plenty of opportunities to uncover the extent of your knowledge.

Convincing People is a Campaign, not a Battle

Radio stations play songs over and over again because repetition sinks the melody in your head. If you gave your loved one a small token of your esteem every week, you'd get far more credit than one large gift at the end of the year. Keeping top of mind is a campaign and not a battle. When one writes a report or pushes an idea, one should have a series of follow-on reports or calls already planned to keep in front of your audience. Another reason why one shouldn't include everything one knows in the first report is that the unused information provides fodder for another report.

Reports are a Selling Document, but Need Balance

When lawyers present a closing argument, they just have to convince the jury that their client is innocent whether they know if the client is guilty or not. The analyst not only has to convince the investor of his point of view, but the idea has to make money for the investor as well. A report that does not offer a balanced view is providing a disservice to the client. As a selling document, the report should include not only the base case but a bull case and bear case. Listing what could go right will excite readers, listing what could go wrong will protect them. When you take exams in college, guessing is fine, but not spelling out clearly what is opinion and facts will jeopardize your credibility, which could be difficult to recover.

Don't Try for A's

Writing a well-researched report takes time, but from the time one comes up with an investment idea and the time the report is written, the market is moving. The longer this period, the more likely the report will be stale by the time it is published. Perfect is the enemy of good. Speed to market is as important as completeness.

Need Numbers to Support the Story

Every report needs numbers to support the conclusions of the report and therefore should include a model. Each company model is unique, so providing a blueprint that covers all stocks is challenging, but from my experience reviewing hundreds of BofA Global Research models, I feel there are certain aspects of models that can be generalized.

Forecasting Revenue Tips

In contrast to economists, who measure quarterly changes sequentially, making seasonal adjustments, Wall Street analysts rely on year-over-year comparisons to neutralize seasonality and the timing of holidays. Seasonal adjustments add a level of complexity that usually doesn't add much value to the analysis of trends in revenue growth, but year-over-year comparisons can be misleading if the year-ago period was somehow unusually strong or weak. I sometimes try to find a year in which business trends were steady and make a quarterly comparison of the base year. In sectors such as technology, analysts simply extrapolate revenues by assuming a gradual deceleration in year over year revenue growth because percentage gains become harder to achieve as the revenue base gets larger. In sectors such as mining/energy, analysts multiply their forecast of production by price, which is often based on prices in the futures market. Consumer staples forecasts are also often based on a price times volume methodology, extrapolating recent price trends for their forecasts after adjusting for inflation.

My preferred method of predicting revenues is to look at the budgets of a company's customers. Of course, forecasting a company's customer budgets is no easier than forecasting a company's revenues, but at least changes in customer budgets provide some warning of a change in a company's revenue trends. For machinery and some chemical stocks, I look at the mining and farmers budgets to predict demand. For personal healthcare and consumer products, consumer incomes are the baseline driver. For technology and capital equipment, changes in corporate profits tend to predict revenue turning points. Some businesses, such as airlines and hotels, have demand-driven equally by business and consumer, but because corporate spending is more volatile than consumer spending, I find that the business budgets are the bigger swing factor. Housing demand is an important driver for home improvement stores, furnishings, fixtures, appliances, and beds. Job growth is the principal engine of growth for business services and commercial real estate, miles driven leads auto repair demand, while the US Defense budget provides several years of visibility on the outlook for defense stocks.

Signs of Overoptimism

Looking at customer budgets provides discipline since the sales from customers can't grow faster than their own spending power for long unless the company is taking customers away from competitors. In fragmented businesses, individual company's revenues do have the opportunity to outpace the market, but the consolidation of most industries in the past decades has made share gains more challenging. A good practice is to add up the revenue forecasts for each of the leading companies since not all companies can gain share. If the revenue growth exceeds nominal GDP growth or the increase in customer budgets, then the forecasts are all probably overly optimistic.

Companies with strong brands can raise prices above inflation for a period of time, but even companies with addicted customers reach a limit. Philip Morris raised prices on its Marlboro cigarettes for two decades, but eventually, the price gap between Marlboro and the more generic brand grew so wide that Marlboro started to steadily lose share. On *"Marlboro Friday"* in 1993, Philip Morris cut its prices 20%, and the stock dropped 26%. To guard against a break in trend, analysts should monitor the price gap against competitors or substitutes. Consumer goods companies like P&G also had to reverse its pattern of steady price gains post 2000 as its price premium to store brands grew too wide, and the prices of chicken, beef and pork are somewhat correlated because families can easily switch to the meat that offers the better value.

Other warning signs could be increases in receivables and inventories. If a company's receivables (amount billed but not collected from customers) start to rise, that could indicate that the quality of customers have deteriorated or finances are tightening among existing customers. Analysts can check the inventory levels of public company customers to determine whether there is overstocking. Globalization has complicated revenue forecasting. Non-US markets account for 30% of the revenues of S&P 500 index so in periods in which the US economy outpaces global growth, the revenue trends of businesses with more foreign exposure will lag the more domestically-focused sectors.

Forecasting Expenses Tips

While revenues are tied to what customers pay, most costs are tied to what a company produces or to the process of securing customers. Most analysts model expenses consistent with how the company reports line items in their financial reports so that they receive continual feedback on the accuracy of their estimates. Breaking down revenues or expenses into too many elements gives a false sense of accuracy. One could try to predict airline revenues by projecting the contribution of every single route, but the margin of error for each estimate would add up and make the final prediction less accurate than a more generalized approach. Similarly, for expenses, sometimes combining line items results in a simpler and more accurate approach.

For most companies, expenses can be divided into the following categories: labor, materials, capital (depreciation, rent and interest expense), sales and marketing, third-party services, and administration costs. Try to uncover the main driver for each expense item, which often starts with calculating a unit of production. Airline analysts use seat-miles (size of plane times miles flown) while other transportation analysts (rails, trucks, shippers) use carloads or shipments. Mining, refining, energy and utility companies focus on the volume or weight of what they produce, while businesses selling directly to consumers usually keep track of volumes sold. Technology, business service, financial service, and internet analysts focus on customers, but sometimes all an analyst has to measure output is revenues.

Using airlines as an example, headcount grows proportionally to the number and size of the planes an airline operates as well as the number of miles the planes fly while increases in compensation per employee (labor expense divided by headcount) is detailed in labor contracts or tied to general inflation. Fuel expense, an airline's most significant material cost, is a function of fuel consumption, which is tied directly to miles flown and fuel price, which can be estimated using futures curve markets. Adjustments can be made to fuel consumption if the fleet is getting older or younger and air traffic delays are increasing or decreasing. Fuel prices can differ from the futures curve if the company has embarked on a hedging program or if one has a strong view of the direction of oil prices.

Airplanes and airport facilities are expensive, and the costs of acquisition can manifest as depreciation and interest expense if purchased outright or rent if leased. Although the method of purchase decisions can determine whether the cost shows up as depreciation, interest or rental expense, the overall capital cost is generally unaffected by the financing choice so I forecast capital costs on a combined basis. Management typically provides a capital spending plan, and I start by assuming the company will own all of the assets. Using the most recent year as a base, I grow capital costs by the additional depreciation resulting from the purchase (planes last for 25 years so I divided capital expenditures by 25), then add the amount of interest expense based on how much the company will have to borrow to finance the purchase, and finally artificially divide the total capital costs back into depreciation, rent and interest expense.

Selling and marketing costs are usually a function of revenues, but technology, financial service, and internet analysts often combine these items to calculate the cost of acquiring a customer. There are some economies of scale in acquiring customers, but at some point, a company has to work harder to find new customers. Internet companies whose customer acquisition costs are rising or much higher than peers probably do not have sustainable business models. In all cases, look to see if the cost of acquiring customers is rising or falling relative to peers.

Third-party services, administration and other costs are frequently tied to units of production as well as outsourcing decisions. Footnotes in the financial statement give a good sense of what causes the book tax rate to deviate from the statutory rate, as well as the difference between book taxes and cash taxes. Lastly, share count should rise over time in line with stock compensation and option exercise minus share repurchase.

Self-checks on Models and Currency Effects

After completing a model, one should conduct some common-sense checks on the model. If year-over-year revenue growth is accelerating or decelerating, one should have an explanation for any change in trend or why revenues can consistently outpace the economy or customer budgets. To determine whether swings in profit are consistent with revenue trends, one should calculate incremental margins. Incremental margins are the increase in profits relative to the increase in revenues. For example, if revenues climb from $1000 to $1200 (a $200 gain) and operating profits rise from $100 to $150 ($50 improvement), then operating margins increase from 10.0% to 12.5%, but the incremental margin is 25% ($50/$200). Companies with high fixed costs tend to have higher incremental margins, but if the model is forecasting an incremental margin that is higher than achieved in previous upturns, the projections are probably too optimistic. Incremental margin analysis should be conducted on estimates that are falling as well as rising - usually margins fall when revenues decline.

Models involving international corporations should also take into account currency fluctuations. Currency changes can have a business impact as well as a translational effect. If a US company has a foreign subsidiary whose revenues and expenses are completely contained within a country or region, then the impact of currencies is purely translational. For example, a European subsidiary with €100mn profits adds $120mn to a US-based corporation's earnings if the US dollar-euro exchange rate is $1.20 per euro, $100mn if the US dollar exchange rate is $1.00 per euro and $140mn if the exchange rate is $1.40 per euro. In other words, a stronger dollar translates into lesser profits and a weaker dollar into more profits for this corporation.

However, the impact becomes more complicated when there is a mismatch between a company's revenues and expenses and currency fluctuations can have a margin impact as well. If the foreign subsidiary happens to export and has a lot of revenues tied to the US dollar, but most of its expenses are in local currencies, a stronger dollar can boost margins enough to offset the translational effect. Imagine that in the prior example, the European subsidiary achieved its €100mn profits with €1000mn of revenue, of which half were generated in US dollars (€500mn is equivalent to $600mn), but all €900mn of expenses were euro-based. If the dollar strengthened from $1.20 to $1.00 per euro, then the subsidiaries euro revenues would rise to €1100mn (€500mn from Europe, but now the equivalent of €600mn from US sales) while expenses would remain €900mn and euro-based profits would total €200mn. Even after the negative translational effect, a stronger dollar in this example would have boosted the subsidiary's contribution by $80mn ($200mn minus $120mn). Conversely, a subsidiary with more revenues denominated in foreign currencies than expenses would suffer from a stronger dollar. If the dollar weakened to $1.40 per euro, revenues would fall to €929mn (€500mn from Europe, but now the equivalent of €429mn from US sales) while expenses would remain €900mn and profits would drop to €29mn ($41mn).

Thematic Research – Stories Drive Stocks

Some of the most successful analysts become renowned by formulating major investment themes (or hopping aboard early) and sticking with them for several years. Thematic work offers several advantages to the analyst:

1) Investors, like most people, relate to stories.

2) Thematic work lends itself to repetition so an analyst's name can be associated with a set of stocks.

3) Because themes play out over time, investors have multiple opportunities to capitalize on these long-term trends.

How Much will Change in a post-COVID World?

In this section, I will discuss some themes whose outcomes I think will determine some of the winners and losers over the next decade. The most immediate issue is what changes from the pandemic are permanent and what will prove temporary. Other issues of importance include whether globalization trends will persist, how inequality will be addressed, can productivity growth be reignited, how governments and companies will respond to climate change, and what could happen if easy monetary policies end. Many of these issues intersect.

The pandemic has clearly upended our personal lives. Some of its effects are temporary, some are permanent, and in some cases, the pandemic has accelerated existing trends. Over time, we are allocating more of our budgets on services relative to goods, but because the pandemic limits personal contact, spending in 2020 and 2021 have favored goods over services. Once we put COVID-19 behind us, spending will once again be directed more towards services like travel, entertainment, personal care, and dental. Pet adoptions may stall, but the pets obtained during the pandemic will keep pet spending high. The trajectory of weddings and births have been in a steady downward path but should stage a temporary post-pandemic rebound. Growing economic inequality has caused the growth in spending from the top quartile to exceed the bottom quartile. This trend reversed during the pandemic, partly because of massive government assistance but also because the wealthy spent more on services. Post-pandemic, the growth in spending among the well-to-do should significantly outpace the growth in spending among the poor.

The long-term pandemic on our working lives is less clear but has important implications for urbanization, transportation, technology, and employee relations. For employees, working from home has increased flexibility in dealing with personal matters while eliminating the cost and time of commuting. On the other hand, some of the spending on technology and sundries (cleaning, toilet paper, office supplies) have shifted to the employee from the company, and the blurred delineation between work and home has probably led to employees working longer hours. Virtual meetings can be effective at maintaining existing relationships but makes building new relationships more difficult. For new employers, training becomes more difficult when you can't watch from the sidelines, listen in on calls, or take calls from clients or suppliers when the boss is gone.

For companies, the option of working from home can be a recruiting tool, and working from home can save money if the company needs less real estate and spends less on maintaining offices. However, savings from hybrid models can be harder to achieve unless employees are willing to share workspaces at a time when COVID-19 has made people wary of sharing their personal space. Perhaps rather than having one's own desk, the company will give each worker their own locker and then the worker can choose any open desk or office. Work's social aspects are important as well as its monetary aspect, and there is a value to physical presence. I would anticipate the current high level of employee turnover to persist in the years ahead if working from home becomes prevalent. In addition to the risk of burnout from working from home, employees working remotely are likely to feel less tied to their company and are freer to look for work elsewhere.

Working from home may widen the inequality gap - higher income individuals are more likely to have better internet and technology as well as more space to separate work from home, particularly those with children. Companies seeking diversity will have to find a way to invest in some of their employee's home technology. Companies may also feel the pressure to increase childhood support or lobby for more government investment in childcare. The difficulty of securing networks becomes more challenging when points of contact are not in a central office but spread over a wide geography and a large number of devices, many of which will be used for personal interactions, thereby putting continued upward pressure on cybersecurity budgets. The shift to the cloud from technology run on-premise is likely to accelerate as more work from home.

The success of virtual conferences certainly offers companies a cost-saving alternative, but I expect business travel to remain the backbone of airlines. Employees who work from home will probably be more desperate for personal contact and opportunities to network at conferences. Companies may feel the increased need to create bonding experiences, which will require employees to fly in from remote locations. Face-to-face meetings also have an intensity that virtual meetings can't replace. Participants are probably multi-tasking when attending virtual meetings - listening but not fully listening. When you are in the same room with someone, you are more likely to have their full attention. Still, the research on whether remote work impedes collaboration is not conclusive.

Automobiles caused a shift in population from the city to suburbs, causing many downtowns to suffer. Technology had initially helped reverse that trend and cities staged a rebound in recent decades as companies valued having access to a concentrated, educated talent pool. Working from home could reverse the urbanization trend, although younger people's desire to congregate still favors cities. Nevertheless, the absence of commuter dollars could have a huge impact on downtown retail and restaurants even in a hybrid environment and the impact on commercial real estate would be devastating in a pure remote world.

The demand for telemedicine surged during the pandemic, and I would expect the shift to remote medical care to continue beyond the pandemic. Virtual medicine makes more efficient use of the pool of doctors and nurses, and many patients don't receive needed routine or timely medical care because of the cost, convenience and difficulty of scheduling and making appointments, particularly in less wealthy communities. While having a personal relationship with a doctor is preferable, more and more of a patient's history is available online, making a remote visit more efficient to the doctor and patient - no more waiting in reception, no more visits to the emergency room for routine care, and earlier care may prevent more serious and expensive outcomes down the road. Artificial intelligence may also permit faster and more accurate readings of scans and other imagery.

E-commerce's share of retail spending has doubled during the pandemic, and even baby boomers have been forced to become more tech-savvy, so I expect the shift away from bricks-and-mortar to continue, albeit at a slower pace. Food rarely looks and tastes as good when taken out, meals are a social occasion as well as nourishment, and the cost of food delivery is much higher than goods so I am more skeptical that the share of takeout food can continue to grow. Price elasticity of takeout has not yet been tested because restaurants were desperate for customers during the pandemic and internet companies are willing to lose money to stimulate sales as long as the stock market rewards growth over profits. Bricks-and-mortar shopping also has a social element that cannot be replaced and opportunities for serendipity (finding things you weren't looking for) that is lacking on the internet (consumer sees what search engine shows them). Still, one can shop in the store and buy online because there is rarely the time element of a meal. Stores are starting to capitalize on their physical presence by becoming marketing rather than selling spaces and appealing to the consumer's desire for experiences. Department stores are creating stores within their stores where a clothing/product maker showcases their goods, as recently evidenced by Disney's shop-in-shop within Target and Toys R Us sections within Macy's stores. This new model favors the larger destination malls relative to the second-tier and strip malls.

Has Globalization Run its Course?

Globalization has shaped the world economies over the past few decades, but a wave of nationalism could result in a slowing or even partial reversal of this trend. The spread of capitalism has lifted hundreds of millions out of poverty in emerging markets but also widened the spread between rich and poor. Globalization has shifted manufacturing jobs from the US and Western Europe to China as well as emerging markets in Asia, Mexico and Eastern Europe, and lower labor costs have contributed to corporations achieving record profit margins. The deflationary effect of globalization has enabled monetary authorities to keep interest rates at historic lows without igniting goods/service inflation but has led to an extended period of asset price inflation, sending the market to record highs and further widening the gap between rich and poor.

Globalization has also enabled companies to play tax arbitrage and corporate tax rates have hit historic lows. Even before corporate tax rates were cut during the Trump administration, US corporate taxes as a percentage of GDP had dropped to around 1% as compared to 4% in the 1950s-1960s. The effective tax rate was only 11% in 2018, well below the US statutory rate of 21%. For book purposes, the drop in the tax rate has lifted earnings by 25% over the past twenty years, contributing to the strong earnings growth that has been a primary driver of higher stock prices. OECD countries, including the US, have arrived at a framework to make it harder for companies to shift their income to countries with lower tax rates. At the very least, corporates are unlikely to enjoy a further boost to earnings via a lower tax rate, and higher corporate tax rates appear likely to pass during the Biden administration.

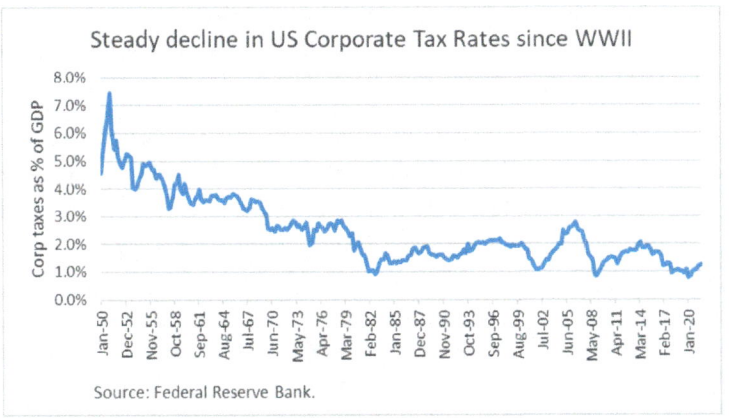

Source: Federal Reserve Bank.

Consumers in the developed economies have benefited from lower prices, but the pressure on wages for less-educated workers has stirred up resentment in US and Europe, sparking a wave of nationalistic fever, which Trump capitalized on during his America First campaign. In addition, China's more muscular foreign policy has made the US more cautious about depending on other countries for critical products, resources and technology, and shortages of equipment during COVID-19 laid bare our dependence on foreign manufacturing. Companies have some economic incentives to partly reverse the globalization of supply chains, particularly as wage gaps have narrowed among countries. Shorter supply chains lower transportation costs, require less management attention, reduce working capital requirements, and enable companies to be nimbler in addressing changes in demand. A greater focus on ESG may also contribute to more localized supply chains, which are likely to be less energy-intensive and subject to stricter worker and environmental regulations.

Whether globalization has run its course could determine the next round of winners and losers. US manufacturing jobs that went to Asia may now come back to the US or move to Mexico and Central America. On the other side of the Atlantic, jobs could return to Western Europe or continue to move to Eastern Europe. Even if jobs return to the continent of their demand, but don't come all the way back to the home market, US and European exports would benefit because Central and Latin American businesses/consumers have a greater propensity to buy from the US than Asian players and Eastern European economies are more likely to buy from Western Europe. Higher pay may crimp corporation profit margins in the US, but would lift demand, which has been held back by wage stagnation. Low factory utilization has curtailed expansion plans, and higher demand could boost capital spending to capture more revenues but would impede corporate cash flow.

Among sectors, industrials will benefit most from greater capital spending, more localized supply chains would help truckers at the expense of shipping and possibly rails as well as more domestically oriented small-cap stocks relative to the larger cap international corporations. The fear of technological dependence will increase demand for semi-cap equipment but may eventually produce duplication of capacity, which could ultimately put pressure on semiconductor prices. Globalization impacted prices of goods more than services, so goods inflation will probably outpace service inflation. For retailers, the cost of basic apparel will rise, but local supply chains may enable them to more quickly adapt to changes in consumer tastes. If the shift in supply chains causes the China export machine to stall, the Chinese government will probably continue its more aggressive foreign policy, and greater distrust and economic competition among nations will spur growth in global defense spending.

Equality

A more connected world appears to create more winner-take-all scenarios for people and businesses. In the industrial revolution, faster and more reliable transportation enabled companies to access a wider market and contributed to the creation of powerful companies, led by immensely rich industry moguls. Today, technology connects people and companies across the globe and has again led to consolidation within industries, dominant companies, and an even richer set of tycoons. Although Democrats cite tax cuts as a factor, the asset bubble created by low rates and monetary authorities purchasing financial assets has had a far greater impact on inequality. Americans have historically been relatively tolerant of inequality as long as they believed that everyone was playing on an equal playing field, but the left is now tapping into the concern that prejudice has held back Blacks, Latinos and women while the right is now tapping into the fears from nonurban areas and non-college grads that the establishment (including government and the media) has stacked the deck against the middle class and working poor.

The challenge for the government is how to split the pie more fairly without shrinking the pie, and these decisions will create winners and losers. Higher tax rates won't significantly impact the very richest Americans because most of their wealth is in appreciating stock, which they either don't need to sell or can raise cash by borrowing against their holdings. However, more progressive tax rates will affect the top wage earners and curb spending of luxury goods. Some Democrats have pushed for a wealth tax, which would hit the richest Americans hardest, but a wealth tax is likely to be considered unconstitutional.

Higher taxes on realized or unrealized capital gains could also be an option, which would impact all stock prices, particularly in the financial sector.

Citing a study by the Swiss Finance Research Institute that calculated 75% of US industries have become more concentrated in the past decade, the Biden administration seeks to reduce the power of large corporations to promote competition and tilt the negotiating balance more in favor of labor. Antitrust laws are likely to be more rigorously enforced but may require a change in mindset as well, which has been based on consumer welfare. How can you claim that consolidation is bad for consumers when products like Facebook and Google search are given away free to the consumer and the economy is seeing little goods or service inflation? Nevertheless, too much power concentrated in too few hands is a recipe for abuse, and the government is likely to continue to seek ways to make sure the public interest is considered; hopefully, interference will be constructive, but sometimes a government cure is worse than the disease.

Equality can be pro-growth if policies untap the potential of disadvantaged groups. Currently, there are record numbers of job openings, many of which are unfilled because of a lack of qualified workers. Companies used to train workers, but now they look to fill openings with people who already have the requisite skills. Government-sponsored training programs are rarely successful, and policies are needed to get on-the-job training for the unemployed. Perhaps for people who have been unemployed for more than a year, the government could split the wage cost with companies for the first six months of employment. The difficulty of finding and affording childcare for dual working parents is impeding productivity, and the government needs to find a way to work with companies to provide affordable care. I expect childcare and worker training to become bigger and more professional businesses in the years to come. Working from home and learning from home requires strong internet service. The pandemic has further laid bare the rich vs poor and urban vs rural technology gap. Federal and state governments are likely to build or subsidize Wi-Fi services in disadvantaged regions, which may impact profits of the communication service providers but provide a further boost to e-commerce and e-learning.

A healthier and better-educated population would also boost growth, but our system has not yet found a way to deliver these services effectively or efficiently. In healthcare, companies that can integrate patient data from all service points and provide analytics to optimize care hold promise but may require the government to force providers to adopt a common technology platform and uniform set of diagnosis/treatment codes. Governments and insurers are experimenting with value-based care, in which providers are paid based on health care outcomes rather than the number of procedures. In education, community colleges, which do appear to be cost-effective ways to raise skill levels for students left behind, may be the best place to direct education dollars.

Productivity Puzzle

Real wages in the US have barely budged in the past twenty years, and faster wage growth would help promote equality but is not sustainable unless accompanied by higher productivity. We all seem to be working harder with fewer resources, but that feeling is unsupported by the economic data. Productivity has edged up slightly more than 1% in the past 15 years as compared to around 3% in prior decades. Factors contributing to sluggish productivity growth include higher security costs, more regulations, lack of corporate investment, greater industry concentration, lower business formation, higher security costs, globalization, labor pool constraints, and transition costs among disrupted industries.

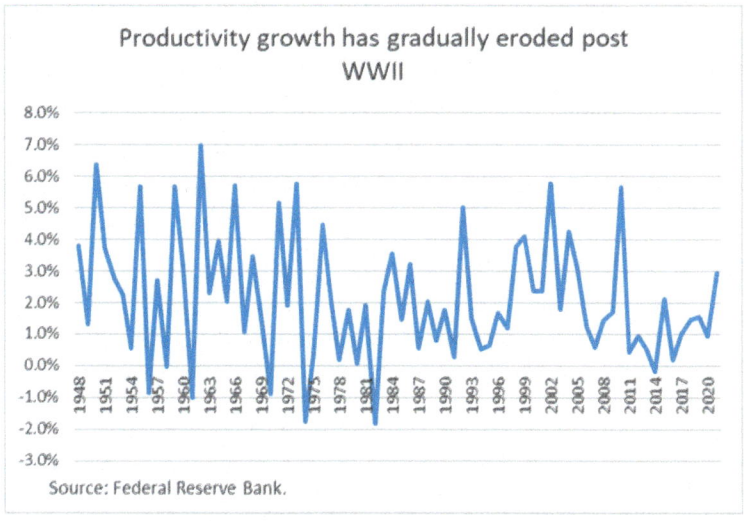

Security Costs Have Escalated

The threat of terrorism post-9/11 has led to a lasting increase in the cost of physical security. As an airline passenger, all I want to do is get on the plane, but the airlines and airports now have hired many employees to stop me - some to check my bags, some to check my ID entering security, some to screen my bags, and some to let me onto the plane. Travelers used to be able to get to an airport within 30 minutes of their flight but now must set aside at least an hour in the larger airports. To enter an office building, one now has to go through security. The benefits of safety are hard to quantify, and the number of people hired to monitor customers/employees/visitors seeking access to buildings and transportation is associated with no new output.

We are also in the midst of a battle to protect ourselves electronically. Like whack-a-mole, whenever we arrest some hackers or create new tools to protect ourselves online, cybercriminals discover new ways to penetrate our networks. Our protection comes at a cost, and the surge in cybersecurity spending does not produce measurable output and has caused productivity to decline in many of the larger enterprise software, networking equipment, internet and utility companies. I do not anticipate either physical or electronic security costs will be declining anytime soon.

Regulatory Protection also Comes with a Cost

The Great Financial Crisis exposed the vulnerability of the global banking system and regulations designed to avoid another crisis, and the largest banks are indeed much stronger, as evident by their resilience during the pandemic. Nevertheless, regulatory protection comes at a cost. As measured by page count, the federal regulatory burden has proliferated more than 60% in the past 20 years and large bank productivity (inflation-adjusted sales per employee) has declined over this time frame. In contrast, regional banks enjoy a much lower regulatory burden, and their productivity climbed sharply during these years.

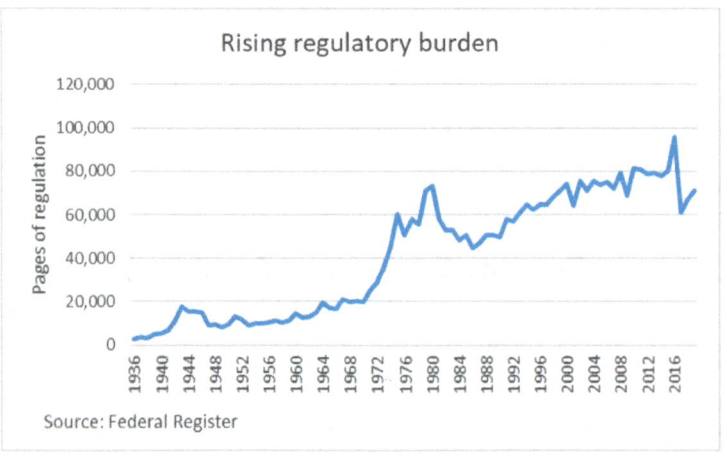

Source: Federal Register

The number of regulations has climbed steadily over the years, with sustained drops only occurring during the Reagan years. Productivity dropped during the 1970s, coinciding with the biggest wave of regulations during the later years of the Nixon and Carter administrations, but rebounded during the 1980s. Productivity took a further dive after the Great Financial Crisis spurred another wave of regulation during the Obama administration. Early in most administrations, there were efforts to cut the regulatory burden, and Trump's administration initially cut red tape by 36%, but the number of regulations climbed sharply later in his administration. Biden has aggressively introduced new rules during his brief time in office, and regulatory page count is one track to exceed the prior peak in 2022. Businesses are less likely to invest when they are uncertain of the rules of the game. Trump's unpredictability probably curbed capital spending during his term, and the recent spike in regulations could restrain investments and productivity gains in the coming decade, particularly for social media, industrials, and service businesses.

Government and Companies Have Not Invested Enough

Lifting productivity requires investment, but US capital spending has been inadequate in both the public and private sectors. After growing at a low double-digit pace for most of last century, Federal government spending on fixed assets has decelerated to a low single-digit pace in the past 30 years. Private capital spending nearly matched depreciation prior to 2000 but has averaged only 80% of depreciation in the past two decades.

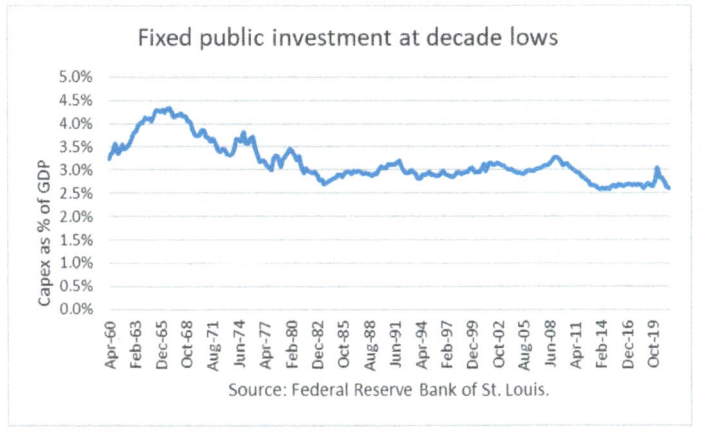

Globalization has probably played a role in keeping US private capital spending low despite record-high margins and cash flow. Why invest in labor savings devices when outsourcing abroad offers a cheap supply of labor? The shift to overseas manufacturing has also channeled capital spending abroad and pushed down plant utilization in the US, lessening the need to expand US capacity. This creates a negative feedback loop in which lower investment leads to lower productivity, leads to slower wage growth, leads to less US demand leads to less need for investment. In addition, companies struggling with globalization and/or technological disruption often suffer declining productivity as demand shrinks faster than headcount during transitions.

However, the outlook for capital spending is now improving. Infrastructure spending has bipartisan support, and the direction of investment is clearly on the rise with only the magnitude in question. As pressures from global outsourcing abate, investing in US manufacturing is getting renewed attention, and the supply of skilled labor is becoming a constraint, exacerbated by the "*silver tsunami*" (baby boom retirements), the opioid crisis, a rising percentage of incarcerated young males, and a lower graduation rate among males versus females. As labor tightness causes wage pressure to rise, companies will have a greater incentive to invest in productivity enhancements, benefiting companies making robotics and other capital equipment.

5G, which offers download speeds 10x-100x faster than existing standards, could be a major driver of capital spending and will probably be adopted faster by businesses than consumers. The Internet of Things (IoT) may transform the image of Industrials as more tech-savvy companies. Embedding equipment with sensors that can communicate with other devices as well as central control could enable factories to quickly locate parts, monitor quality, pinpoint breakdowns and even schedule maintenance prior to any predicted mechanical breakdowns. However, the range of 5G cell towers is less than one-third of a mile as compared to around 30 miles for 4G. 5G will require the building of a lot more towers than before, impacting the cash flow of wireless providers, but benefiting cell tower REITs like American Tower, Crown Castle and SBA Communications as well as 5G equipment providers such as Ericsson, Nokia, Qualcomm, and CommScope.

Autonomous vehicles require the fast reaction time of 5G and are more likely to be first implemented in long-haul truck routes, which are more predictable than local roads. Autonomous trucks could solve the trucking industry's chronic driver shortages and improve vehicle utilization since computers don't get tired like humans. IoT is already applicable for smart homes, smart buildings, and smart cities as a means of enhancing security and energy efficiency. IoT in farming equipment can save both water and energy and maximize crop yields. 5G for consumer health devices enable continuous monitoring of a patient's heart, glucose and other vital signs and can even turn the toilet into a diagnostic instrument.

Consolidation Improves Efficiency, not Innovation

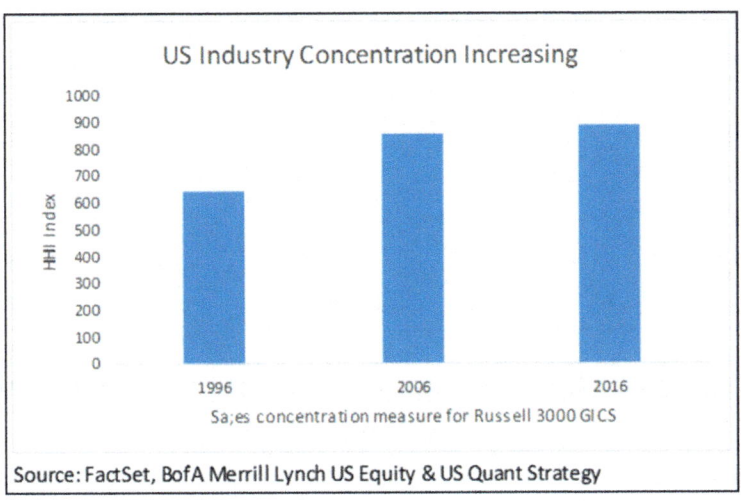

Source: FactSet, BofA Merrill Lynch US Equity & US Quant Strategy

The Herfindahl-Hirschman index, a measure of market concentration, has gained around 40% in the past 25 years and 75% of industries are more consolidated today during that time frame. New business formation stalled over the past two decades, averaging 20% below pre-2000 levels, but have jumped in 2020-2021, possibly related to COVID. These trends have had a negative impact on productivity. New businesses tend to be much more innovative than established firms as evident by the need for large tech companies like Facebook, Google, Microsoft and Salesforce to acquire smaller companies that have developed technologies that the mega-caps could not develop on their own. Larger companies are generally better at optimizing existing products and improving efficiency than revolutionary change. The benefits of disruption are much less for companies that already have large market shares. Culture is also a factor as established companies have larger bureaucracies and an ingrained way of doing things. Witness the struggles of the global auto companies, which despite their engineering talent and experience, have yet to catch up to Tesla in electric vehicle sales thirteen years after Tesla introduced its first model. Efforts by the Biden Administration to more strictly enforce antitrust laws could boost productivity if coupled with a jump start in new business formation through investment banking M&A revenues would suffer. With so many mergers involving companies that act across borders, pushback on combinations could also come from foreign governments as well.

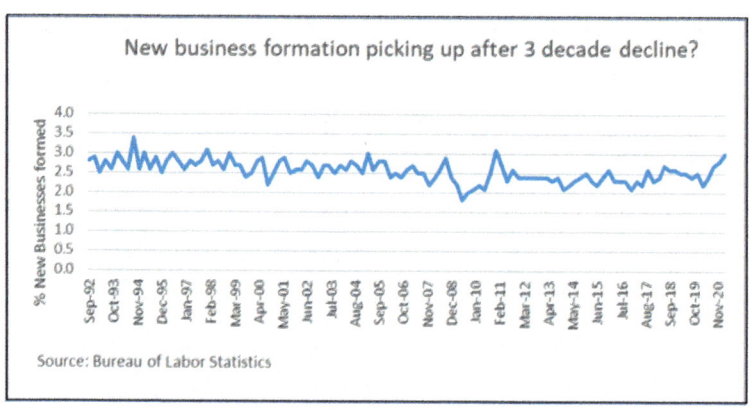

Addressing Climate Change Good for People, but not Productivity

While there are still naysayers, the consensus among Corporate America is that rising greenhouse gas levels are causing temperatures to rise, and action needs to be taken whether to comply with government regulations or demands from their own constituents. There is much less agreement on what actions need to be taken or what policies would be most effective. Fossil fuels are inexpensive and efficient, so substitution with other energy sources or a tax on carbon will raise costs and impact margins for many businesses, especially if not enacted globally. By outsourcing manufacturing abroad, the US and Europe have been indirectly exporting environmental issues into countries with less strict environmental regulations, so while a reversal of globalization raises costs, a shift in production to countries with tougher rules could help the global environment.

The travel industry would have the most difficult time adjusting to changes in pricing carbon. Battery technology is slowly improving to power cars and trucks, but biofuels and electric engines for airplanes seem a lot farther off. Given the sensitivity of demand to price, steep taxes on airline fuel could significantly impact long-haul travel, affecting hotels and the entire global tourism industry as well as the airlines and cruise ships.

The advantage of rails over trucks on long-haul routes would become even larger if fuel was more heavily taxed though electrification may prove easier for trucks than rails as batteries improve.

On the other hand, if engines can be run on hydrogen rather than batteries, travel becomes much cleaner though hydrogen is still energy-intensive to make and is more flammable and less condensed than jet fuel. Hydrogen-based engines favor industrial gas companies like Air Products, whereas electrified vehicles boost demand for minerals, benefiting lithium and copper miners. Nevertheless, hydrogen technology is still in its early stages, and new aircraft designs can take more than a decade to gain FAA approval. Biofuels would not require new engine design and appear the fastest way to make airlines more carbon neutral, but energy companies have yet been able to mass-produce algae-based fuels, which are energy-intensive and multiple times more costly than jet fuel.

In addition to vehicles, the most important part of battery development lies in energy storage. Renewable energies like wind and solar are not produced consistently throughout the day and year and larger and more efficient batteries would store the excesses during peak production to make renewables a more reliable source. Utilities charge their customers based on formulas tied to their energy investments, and the transition to a less carbon-intensive economy will require significant capital spending, which could accelerate utility revenue and profit growth. However, governments may need to subsidize rising energy bills if they squeeze lower-and-middle income families. Climate change appears to be increasing the frequency and intensity of storms that knock out electricity. The investment required by utilities to protect their grid may also put pressure on consumer budgets. In addition, more frequent and severe storms pose a threat to insurance companies if they have not properly priced their services to account for the greater risk.

The OECD estimates that agriculture directly (methane from animal flatulence and rice paddy cultivation, nitrous oxide from fertilizer, manure and urine) and indirectly (cutting down trees, land use) contribute roughly one-quarter of global greenhouse gas emissions. Absorbing the environmental cost would raise the cost of meat and dairy, favoring meat substitutes like Beyond Meat, which are currently more expensive and higher in salt, and milk substitutes. Almond milk is lowest in calories, but less nutritious, requires more water, and is costlier than soy milk. Oat Milk has the creamiest texture of plant-based milk, but is most caloric and expensive. The need to reduce fertilizer poses a long-term threat to top producers CF Industries and Mosaic, but an opportunity for companies producing smarter seeds (Bayer, Corteva, Syngenta) and fertilizer substitutes. For example, startup Pivot Bio is engineering nitrogen-fixing bacteria that would supply nitrogen directly to plant roots without the need for fertilizer. Investments in smarter farming equipment would benefit Deere, Caterpillar, and CNH.

The investment required to redesign plants to improve energy efficiency and cut down waste as well as rebuild our infrastructure to reduce water leakage and minimize energy loss on the grid offer industrials potentially large markets. The need for smart homes and factories creates sizable demand for new products and software. Sharing of resources is pro-environment and encompasses ride-sharing services like Uber, home-sharing services like Airbnb, and infrastructure as service providers, including data centers. Cryptocurrencies like Bitcoin consume huge amounts of energy because transactions are based on proof of work and require tremendous computing power, but there are more energy-friendly options, and Ethereum plans on switching its cryptocurrency to a proof of ownership validation of transactions, which the founder claims will reduce energy consumption by 99%. The outlook for plastics is also mixed. Plastics add to landfills and pollute our oceans, but prevent food waste and have lower transportation costs than substitutes. Plastics are harder to recycle than glass, metal or paper, but investment in collection infrastructure and regulations requiring more uniform composition could lift plastic recycling rates.

Easy Money has Defied Monetarist Theory

In the aftermath of the Great Financial Crisis, the world's monetary authorities have slashed interest rates to unprecedented levels and embarked on multiple rounds of quantitative easing, in which the central banks lower the cost of public and private debt by purchasing securities. Central banks have again acted aggressively to offset the financial impact of COVID-19 and the US money supply is 23% higher in 2021 than 2019 - double prior peak growth rates. Monetarists believed that the velocity of money (the speed money moves through the economy) is relatively constant and expanding the supply of money boosts output, inflation or both. In the 1970s, easy money was associated with stagflation - higher prices despite anemic growth, but that relationship has broken down this century. Despite a prolonged period of easy money, the economy has posted steady though sluggish growth with minimal inflation.

Whether easy money can persist will depend on whether inflation remains subdued and the velocity of money continues to decline. Inflation has picked up in 2021, but mainly as a result of pandemic-related supply disruptions that could prove temporary. The velocity of money is tied to how quickly financial companies lend money out and how fast consumers/businesses spend it. Post-crisis, Dodd-Frank forced larger banks to set aside more reserves for lending, which caused their cost of lending advantage relative to nonbanks to rise 1-2pts from pre-crisis levels, which served to narrow credit spreads and discourage lending growth. As a result of their capital strength, consumers now perceive the large banks as much safer than other alternatives and deposits at the larger banks are at record levels. Therefore, money that is being created is moving to banks that are slower to recycle the money. Meanwhile, the asset bubble created by easy money has helped the wealthy relative to poor, yet the rich have a lower propensity to spend and corporates have been more focused on buying back stock than boosting capital spending.

Non-bank lending was crushed during the Financial Crisis, but has steadily recovered over the past decade and could lift the velocity of money; on the other hand, cryptocurrencies are more likely to take money out of circulation and depress velocity. In regard to spending, as labor markets tighten owing to reshoring of production and a shrinking worker pool, wage growth could lift consumer spending. Corporate spending could finally get a lift as capacity utilization rises and governments spend more on infrastructure. The battle of inflationary versus disinflationary forces will be a key determinant of how long the bull market in assets last. In conclusion, sustained slow, steady, deflationary growth has favored financial over real assets, passive over active investing, growth versus value, and rich versus poor, but the end of easy money could be disruptive to the stock market and reshuffle the winners and losers.

Roles of an Analyst

Lawyer

This book was designed to give investors a framework for analyzing stocks as well as provide companies with a perspective regarding how they are viewed by Wall Street. I also hope that my passion for investing inspires younger people to consider Investment Research as a career, and so I will conclude this book with an attempt to discuss the various roles a sell-side research analyst performs. What is the skill set required of an analyst? In my 40 years of experience, I have found that the job comprises the elements of five professions: lawyer, teacher, salesperson, consultant and entrepreneur. Much of the book has focused on the first role – making an investment case. Making sound investment decisions is not productive if one cannot convince the portfolio manager to buy or sell the stock. Just as a good lawyer needs to understand the makeup of the jury in order to tailor a closing argument, an analyst needs to understand the client's investment process to tailor a stock pitch. Designing a presentation to a growth investor should be different than to a value investor. And like a good lawyer, an analyst needs to capture the audience's attention, so a degree of showmanship is important.

Teacher

A sell-side analyst is a specialist in his field, but our clients are generalists. There is also a fair amount of turnover among the clients as our buy-side counterparts often switch sectors, and the average hedge fund lasts only three years. Consequently, the analyst job has a large teaching component, and since the clients receive individual attention, there is a large amount of repetition in the job as one gives the same explanation over and over again to different people. Attention spans are getting shorter, and people can only absorb so much at one time, so the analyst cannot afford to overload a client with too much information and, like a good lecturer, needs to be somewhat entertaining. Companies often meet with our buy-side clients, who want to look smart and well-informed in front of management. Sell-side analysts often provide buy-siders with a list of questions to ask as well as laying out key business drivers.

Salesperson

Nearly all jobs have a sales component. For investment research, the product being sold is one's own expertise. As in sales, knocking on more doors creates more opportunities for finding someone who wants your project, so analysts try to reach out to as many people as possible. At first, this led to clients being overwhelmed by paper reports, and next came faxes. Then analysts started to fill up client voicemails, and currently, buy-side clients have to sift through hundreds of emails a day. Instant messaging may be the next channel stuffed. More and more, breaking through the clutter has become a challenge, making it harder for new analysts without a reputation to garner attention.

Consultant

Despite Wall Street being viewed as too short-term oriented, the best analysts typically have a long-term vision of where the industry is headed. Information is a two-way street. Companies inform analysts about current business conditions and strategies, but managements also learn from analysts. While management has inside knowledge, the analyst has opportunities to speak with all competitors and acquire a broader perspective. Given the desire of start-ups and young innovative companies to access capital markets, sell-side analysts may be aware of new threats and disruptive technologies quicker than the companies. Buy-side analysts often seek the opinion of company management when choosing sell-side analysts, and managements often recommend the analysts who provide them with the greatest insights.

Entrepreneur

The equities business is relatively fragmented. The top firm has only a low-teens market share, and the commission share of the top five investment banks is less than 50%. Therefore, an analyst who garners 20% of mind share is an industry leader, and niche strategies can be quite successful. Some top-rated analysts are great to stock pickers, but many are not. Instead, some clients look for analysts who are great modelers or sources of industry data. Some choose analysts with the strongest relations with management or those with broader industry connections that can provide a complete perspective. Some choose analysts who are industry visionaries, but others choose analysts owing to their regulatory or accounting expertise. Because sell-side analysts publish their views, clients can easily gauge Wall Street sentiment, but monitoring the buyer-side consensus is more challenging. One of the most common questions clients ask sell-side analysts is, *"What are other buy-side analysts doing?"* An analyst who can make himself the hub of information or views provides a valuable service. Like any entrepreneur, there are many paths to success, and each analyst must decide where his/her individual strength lies.

Made in the USA
Las Vegas, NV
20 June 2022